YOURSELF
OR SOMEONE
LIKE YOU

A SELF-HELP MEMOIR AND JOURNEY
TOWARDS TRAUMA WISDOM

Printed in Australia
Cover and internal design by Shawline Publishing Group Pty Ltd
Images in this book are copyright approved for Shawline Publishing Group Pty Ltd
Illustrations within this book are copyright approved for Shawline Publishing Group Pty Ltd

First Printing: June 2023

Shawline Publishing Group Pty Ltd/New Found Books
www.shawlinepublishing.com.au/new-found-books/

Paperback ISBN 978-1-9229-9319-9
eBook ISBN 978-1-9229-9324-3

Distributed by Shawline Distribution and Lightningsource Global

 A catalogue record for this work is available from the National Library of Australia

More great Shawline titles can be found by scanning the QR code below.
New titles also available through Books@Home Pty Ltd.
Subscribe today at www.booksathome.com.au or scan the QR code below.

YOURSELF
OR SOMEONE
LIKE YOU

A SELF-HELP MEMOIR AND JOURNEY
TOWARDS TRAUMA WISDOM

GRANT PARKIN

DEDICATIONS

Dedicated to those who have loved and lost. Who have experienced trauma and been daunted and jaded by what life has thrown their way. To those who have suffered and thought they could not continue, and yet somehow still have. I salute you. We are all in this together.

To my wife Emma and daughters Lola and Pearl, I am forever grateful to share my life with you.

To my mum and brother Richard, who experienced these traumas with me, and Mum in particular, who has experienced many, many more.

ACKNOWLEDGEMENTS

I would like to acknowledge St Andrew's College and the Rowing Club in particular. I could not give these institutions enough credit for helping mould the man I have become and continue to strive to be. Nec Aspera Terrent.

Similarly, I acknowledge the members of the Rhodes University Rowing Club, particularly 1997 – 1999, who were my friends in the darkest hours.

CONTENTS

Introduction vii

Chapter One - TRAUMA ONE – Mauled by a Dog 1

Chapter Two - Summer of Discontent......................................12

Chapter Three - Six Weeks in 1996 18

Chapter Four - Early University 33

Chapter Five - TRAUMA TWO – Car Crash.............................44

Chapter Six - Life After Dad 54

Chapter Seven - Back to East London 66

Chapter Eight - TRAUMA THREE – Leaving My Homeland.......77

Chapter Nine - Big Red Migration..87

Chapter Ten - TRAUMA FOUR – Betrayal 102

Chapter Eleven - Fraser Island and a Future Unwritten 115

Chapter Twelve - 2011 and Onwards and Upwards 125

Conclusion 132

Epilogue 139

Appendix One 142

Book References 147

INTRODUCTION

My drive to write a book first took hold in the year 2000, the beginnings lost on a hard drive over the years. It was less than two years after the second major trauma experience of my life – the loss of my father in a car accident, when I was nineteen. My mum and brother sustained significant injuries in the event, while I walked away with superficial wounds.

The book I began writing then was very much biographical, as opposed to what you are reading now. A history of the Parkin family in the Eastern Cape or some such theme. Part of the reason it did not progress was my lack of belief that it would be of value to anyone. Perhaps a deep-seated insecurity and feeling of me, (and by proxy the book) being unworthy, however unjustified.

The book you are reading now describes four personal traumas and the choices I have made in dealing with them[1]. I was mauled by a dog at the age of three, experienced the car accident at age nineteen, emigrated in my late twenties and was betrayed by my

---

[1] I have changed some names in recounting these stories. It is just easier that way. Where relevant, I have reproduced details from the journals I kept, while others are based on what I can remember of the period, in consultation (where practical) with friends who were with me at the time.

wife in my early thirties. Documenting these events has been scary and confronting. I have grown immensely since taking on the responsibility for detailing them. Choosing to revisit the darkest periods of my life and their impact on me, my family and my relationships. Transposing thoughts to words and then onto a computer screen. Reviewing journals and sifting through dusty memory boxes. The endless reviews of my own work before it even got to the formal editing. I refined these stories through this process.

They became <u>my</u> stories.

Stories I no longer fear to share. Stories that I am responsible for. Stories I own.

I believe I have now created a book worth reading.

This memoir also contains more than a sprinkling of humour. There is, after all, a real danger of taking this life too seriously. The first print will be published twenty-five years since the anniversary of Dad's passing. No doubt one of the reasons I chose to write it in the first place. Twenty-five years is a long time, and yet it can seem like yesterday. But muddied waters do settle. Clear water provides a far better reflection. This takes time.

Despite these events, I have chosen to consider myself very fortunate and am grateful for the opportunity to share what I have experienced. And it is a choice to feel this way. I am responsible for my state of mind.

Inevitably, writing this book required significant introspection and an attempt to answer the question of 'Who is Grant?'

And who am I? I am a son, a brother, a father, and a husband. I am a friend, a Chartered Accountant, a surfer and a skateboarder. I am a reformed Ironman triathlete. I was a competent oarsman. I was a violinist. Now I play the guitar. I am a migrant and I co-host a podcast in which we discuss the musical composition of albums. I am a survivor... and I have physical (and mental) scars from multiple traumas. All these external validations... Above all else, I am a human being with an ambition to be a better person today than the one I was yesterday. It is my sincerest hope that through reading this memoir you will feel the same ambition. Now let's get cracking.

CHAPTER ONE

TRAUMA ONE – MAULED BY A DOG

I was mauled by a dog when I was three years old.

It was 31 May 1981 at Blanco Guest Farm in the Eastern Cape of South Africa. My parents (Phil and Patty) thought that our young family should take advantage of the public holiday long weekend and get out of the city. The guest farm three hours' drive from home seemed just the tonic. Despite intending to return home a day early due to poor weather, the sun came out that Sunday morning and we decided to stay. After lunch, Dad went off to play bowls while Mum, my little brother Richard and me stayed in our room playing until it was time for afternoon tea. All meals were served at the meal room only a short walk away. The three of us arrived an hour early, having misread the Sunday meal schedule, and decided to go watch Dad. We took a shortcut to the bowling green, walking around the meal room and past the kitchen. Richard was in the pram and I was walking next to Mum, holding a piece of thatch, when the Rhodesian Ridgeback peered out the kitchen door. Mum watched in horror as the dog rushed at me and started attacking, knocking me off my feet. Mum ran forward and tried to beat the dog off me but by then the animal had bitten my forehead, ripped my bottom lip in half and started on the left-hand side of my face. We discovered later that it had previously attacked other children.

(I think) I remember parts of the experience:

The dog turning.

The mouth coming towards me.

Me falling backwards… into darkness.

Hysterical, Mum picked me up and carried me to find help, leaving Richard crying in his pram where the attack had just taken place. Looking back, we were fortunate the dog did not attack him too. One of the other guests saw us covered in blood and rushed to call my dad. There followed some quick decision-making. There was no time to pack belongings and Richard was left with friends while Mum and Dad raced me to Queenstown – the closest large town and over an hour's drive away.

I regained consciousness and was being cradled by Mum in the back seat of our car, blood on the roof and all over my clothes. Sore and in pain. Fear and shock on my dad's face as he turned around from the front passenger seat.

The doctor in Queenstown bandaged my head and gave me something to ease the pain. Dad drove the rest of the way home, still over two hours away, where our family doctor was waiting at the hospital. The legal speed limit was totally ignored as he rushed to get his injured son to safety. Unfortunately, the local plastic surgeon was also away for the long weekend so our doctor offered to stitch up the injuries. It broke Mum's heart when he took me in his arms and walked off to the operating theatre, me screaming desperately for her.

I remember the high roof of a white room. A man in a white coat walking past the doorway with a pen and paper, obviously a doctor, looking in at me, shaking his head and moving on. My eyes black and blue, arms tied to the cot to stop me pulling out my drip. Trapped, sore, alone and afraid. The horrible antiseptic smell of the hospital entering my lungs with every breath, permeating my entire existence.

I needed a skin graft to help fix the wound in between my eyes and had more lacerations on my temple. On the rare occasion I got angry, that scar on my temple, in particular, would get red like Harry Potter's, although this comparison would only be made decades later. It took many stitches to put my face together again.

This was part of how my world view was formed.

Bad things can happen and can happen very quickly. Shortly after leaving the hospital, I snuck into the lounge room where my parents were entertaining friends. I climbed onto some bar stools and subsequently fell off, cracking open the stitches and requiring additional surgery. The last of the reconstruction operations was to remove scar tissue from my bottom lip when I was thirteen.

Immediately after those early operations, I was told not to smile. Smiling would split the stitches holding my bottom lip together. Smiling physically hurt. A child does not understand these concepts. I wanted to laugh and smile. The world was confusing. I cannot imagine how this experience impacted my mum's world view.

On another occasion, I walked out of sight of my parents while wandering around the garden. Our family dog (a golden retriever called Bumpy) gently put my arm in her mouth and led me back within sight. Bumpy's loving care brought back terrible memories and fear in me.

The scars ensured the standard playground name-calling at school: 'Scarface' being chief among them. Having had such an extreme experience so young put me at a disadvantage when it came to dealing with these periods. I was/remain a scar face. I was scared to engage in playground scuffles that might quickly have resolved these episodes of teasing. I knew what pain was. Real physical pain. And real emotional pain. It didn't matter that my parents loved me dearly. These were the facts. Scarface.

At junior school at Selborne Primary in East London[2] (South Africa – yes, it does exist) I meandered through the grades, daydreaming the days away doing just enough to get through and never particularly achieving anything. I played cricket in the summer months and soccer in winter as rugby was too violent for me. People got injured playing rugby. I knew hurt. I did not want to hurt again. In a strange twist of fate, I would break my ankle playing soccer. As there was no such thing as soccer in high school at that time, at least not in the schools I was going to attend, Dad thought it wise that I got a year of rugby under the belt prior to commencing high school. In my last year in junior school, I would play rugby as my winter sport.

I had to make a choice of what position to play in this new sport, which required going on the guidance of the other boys who had played it for years. My body shape lent itself to two positions: 'Inside Centre' (in the backline) or 'Hooker' (in the forwards). As speed and a sidestep were attributes I had never possessed, Centre was out. That left Hooker. In the middle of the front row of the scrum. The scrum: where eight of my mob pushes against eight of your mob for brief ownership of a piece of leather. Hooker: the most dangerous position of the eight, as both your hands grip around the 'Prop' on either side of you. If the scrum collapses, which happens occasionally, you literally eat dirt. People have broken their necks in the scrum[3]. Bad things can happen. I didn't want bad things to happen to me again.

---

[2] East London is a city on the east coast of South Africa, about two-thirds of the way up between Cape Town and Durban.

[3] A local high school boy playing in the front row had broken his neck and died over this period too, no doubt adding to the anxiety of playing Hooker, indeed, in the front row, at all.

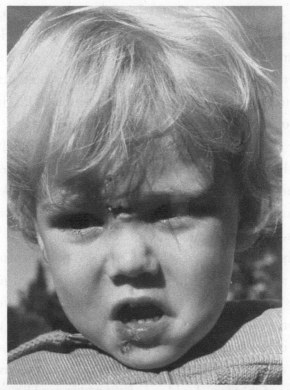

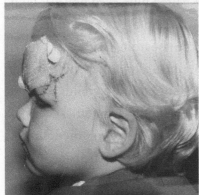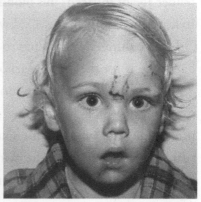

I was mauled by a dog at the age of three. It would be decades before
I fully understood the impact this had on my world view, thanks to reading
Bessel van der Kolk's book *The Body Keeps the Score*. Refer to Appendix One.

With neither option being palatable, I chose option C: 'Loosehead Prop', immediately to the left of the Hooker in the scrum and still in the front row. This allowed me to simply move out of the way if the scrum collapsed. I would play for the under thirteen C team, barefoot in those days. Playing up in Queenstown on frostbitten fields was an experience.

Junior school almost complete, I was going to attend Selborne College the following year. Then my parents went to a presentation for St Andrew's College (based in Grahamstown[4] – 180 kilometres away) late in 1991. My dad[5] and great-grandad had attended St Andrew's, a school so confident it refers to itself only as 'College'. Due to the high cost of the school fees, it was initially planned that I would attend only the final three years (as opposed to the full five years) of high school at College. However, my parents were very impressed with the presentation and I was awarded a bursary, partially covering the costs. My career as an 'Andrean' (scholar at College) commenced in January 1992 in Graham House. At the tender age of thirteen, this blonde-haired blue-eyed boy was going to leave the family home. Dad was unemployed at the time.

I think thirteen was young to go to boarding school, yet others had done it for their whole school careers and knew no different. You do what you have to do, I suppose. I would continue meandering through, spending some time playing cricket, which really didn't hold my attention, and then swimming the following year. Rugby, in the main for winter. Merely a participant. All the while, Dad said I should try rowing.

---

[4] Grahamstown, now called Makhanda is a city of approximately 140,000 people. A number of well-respected educational institutions are based there, including Rhodes University and various private schools. It also used to host the South African National Arts Festival each July.

[5] Dad was in Graham House from 1964 –1968.

January 1992 – My first day at College.
No doubt one of Dad's proudest moments.

Begrudgingly, in January 1994 I attended my first Rowing Camp in Port Alfred[6], sacrificing part of my school summer holiday to row up and down the Kowie River for seven to ten days before the Easter term started. I was late on the rowing scene, having attempted cricket and swimming in those first two years at College. And just to be clear, before the age of fourteen, I had never been good at anything. I also did not want to go to camp.

These guys were weird (and smelly). They were on another planet. I mean seriously, who gives up a week of summer holidays just to remain competitive with the mighty Johannesburg crews? And they wore these weird tights/flannel towelling shorts that left little to the imagination.

Anyway, I was going to try this rowing thing properly and if it was rubbish, my parents were at Kleinemonde[7], a mere sixteen kilometres away. They could pick me up if this didn't work out. I could walk up to the payphone outside Guido's restaurant and call them, and they would come and get me.

Now, rowing attracted a relatively small group of people at the school. It could be the dedication and commitment required, or the horrific hand callouses and 'boat bite'[8]. It could be the pain of racing – you suffer whether you win or lose – or the lack of stylish kit, or the travel requirements, moving heavy boats, washing them down; the list is endless. There are a myriad of reasons why it isn't more popular. Maybe because it can be just plain tough.

Nevertheless, as luck would have it, I made a crew at that camp

---

[6] Port Alfred is a small coastal town with a population of 26,000 and is almost equidistant to East London to the east and Port Elizabeth (PE) to the west, approximately 150 kilometres from each larger city.

[7] Kleinemonde is a small coastal holiday village on the East London side of Port Alfred. We had a family holiday home there since the early 1990s.

[8] A nasty occurrence on your calves, caused by your legs hitting the runners that the rowing seat slides on.

– the U15 AVIII. The fact that there were only eight rowers in our age group was a bonus! And so I rowed. Up and down the Kowie river in the Number Four seat of the boat, with my new mate Jay in at Number Three. We would row twice a day and it was AWESOME! We would wake up early and the water was always flat with fish jumping and only the occasional water skier coming past. Afternoon sessions were generally a bit choppier with the wind up and a few more people out on the water.

In between rowing sessions, we were free to do as we pleased, which sometimes meant sleeping, but most times meant boogie boarding at Port Alfred's famed West Beach. Nick, another new crew mate and I would egg each other into the dumping waves, often after the sun had set. It was highly amusing seeing Nick eating his own gums after tasting the sand bank one day, but that is another story.

About halfway through my first camp, the coach (Matt – an old Andrean[9]) who hardly ever said anything in any of the sessions (probably because he was horribly hung over every morning) asked us to stop rowing and for Jay and me to move from the 'Engine Room'/'Ejector Seat' positions of Three and Four to the Stroke and Seven positions. What?

I had joined an unbeaten crew that had not lost a race as an VIII (or the A IV) – including South African (SA) Champs since they started rowing a year earlier. Now, a few days into the camp, Jay and I were moved to the front of the boat to set the rhythm for the crew. Excitement was one word you could use. Fear was another.

Just because Matt was trialling us in these positions did not mean that we would stay there. But stay we did. Then we were told that Selborne College was coming to the Kowie that weekend

---

[9] Someone who attended College.

for a hastily arranged pre-season regatta.

Selborne, where I went to primary school, was a virtual sworn enemy of College. I would be racing many of my old classmates, stroking the boat in an unbeaten crew. Jay and I were nervous. In fact, nervous was not the word. We were petrified.

We were rookies, and Selborne had run the crew close on a few occasions. How could we ensure that first loss didn't rest on our shoulders? We decided to do the most practical thing… we would jump the start.

Late on a January Saturday afternoon on a wind-swept Kowie River, after multiple attempts by the judges to line us up correctly, we jumped the start, got up by three-quarters of a length and held that gap all the way home.

It was my first medal. Dad gave it to me and Mum captured the moment in a photo that is still up in the lounge room. Selborne was livid. Jay and I didn't care.

I was good at something.

*

That U15 crew would grow in confidence and remain unbeaten until the final regatta of the season – SA Champs. We got smashed that weekend, with both the U15 VIII and U15 A IV losing for the first time in two years. Hindsight provides 20/20 vision and, while very painful at the time and for months to come, I believe we lost for a number of reasons, including:

- A late crew change in both the VIII and the A IV
- My promotion to the A IV with less than 2 kilometres training
- Not having our normal coach at the event
- The crew not turning up mentally on the day

Overall, I had found something I was good at and looked forward to rowing in the second VIII in my first year of the open division the following season, and then in the first VIII in my final year of school. It all looked like it was going to plan, rowing in the second VIII for the end-of-year regattas (Swartkops and Mayor's Plate) in late 1994. However, you know what they say about best-laid plans.

My first rowing medal. I remember being embarrassed by my mum taking that picture. I am so grateful now.

CHAPTER TWO

SUMMER OF DISCONTENT

I was dropped. My name wasn't there.

Could it have been a mistake? Should I talk to the coaches? Surely no mistake had been made – I had been in the crew in the morning session and now I wasn't.

It was January Rowing Camp in Port Alfred, 1995. I would not row in the second VIII for the rest of the season. Little did I know what would transpire as a result of Coach Luke dropping me that day. Maybe I had been more naturally fit one year earlier. Maybe I shouldn't have eaten a Magnum ice cream most days before the 1995 Camp. Maybe I believed my rowing report card too much and grew complacent. It was all irrelevant now as I spent the rest of the season wallowing in the third VIII with people who didn't take rowing as seriously as me.

The only good session of the year was when Jeremy coached us one afternoon on Settlers Dam. He stated from the coaching pontoon that I was the most talented in the crew and to follow me. Jeremy was a massive physical specimen, had won the Grand Challenge at the Buffalo Regatta[10] and rowed for Rhodes

---

[10] The Buffalo Regatta is held in East London on the Buffalo River. It is South Africa's biggest rowing regatta. It has been held every year since 1881 (except for an interruption during the war years and 2021 due to the Covid pandemic). Made from pure silver and deemed

University and South Africa. He had a ponytail too – he was cool!

However, one off-handed positive comment wasn't enough to keep me rowing, and I wanted out. I wanted out real bad. I didn't want to row, I did not want to go to SA Champs, I just wanted to leave the whole thing alone.

I spent many a night in the tickie box (phone booth) in Graham House discussing exit strategies and options with my parents. I just wanted to have fun and enjoy my sport. Rowing in the third VIII was not fun. I wanted to quit rowing to go and play water polo – to enjoy my last year of high school with my mates.

My parents did what any good parents would do. They suffered with me, listened to my rants of unhappiness and then offered wisdom.

'If you leave rowing now, you will give up all the progress you have made and have to learn another sport. Chances are you will have the same third VIII experience in the water polo pool or the cricket pitch. Why don't you row the rest of the season, really train hard in the off-season and arrive at the January Camp super, super fit and see how it goes? If you really apply yourself, you may get a very different result.'

Well, that eventually (I say eventually because it took a while) got through to me. All I knew was that I could never row for a crew like that again. I wanted to row with a crew who wanted to race. And win.

*

---

priceless, the trophies for the Buffalo Grand Challenge (for Senior-A Coxless Fours) and the Silver Sculls (for Senior-A Single Sculls) races are regarded as the most valuable in Southern Africa for any sport.

I chose to stay with rowing and give it my best crack at making the first VIII the following season. I was to be responsible for my fate. I needed to own the story, even if the outcome I wanted now seemed unlikely. I even went so far as to make a poster above my bed with the minimum distance required on the Derrick Read rowing ergometer machine to be eligible for the first VIII. There were no Concept 2s (now the world standard in rowing ergometers) in the Eastern Cape Province yet... we were old school. The sign read: 'First Team 8.2'. That sign was the first thing I saw every morning when I woke up and was the last thing I saw when I went to sleep.

After a very indifferent SA Rowing Champs, my summer of discontent was turning into my autumn of (even more) discontent as rugby season started. My feeling of 'not being good enough' and being afraid of getting hurt or injured permeated onto the rugby field as well. As a result, I was lumped into the fifth to seventh team squad. There were no teams below this squad in the open division. It was an interesting day at practice on Webster Field as the frustrations of it all were really getting to me. Playing in a shitty trial match on this dust bowl of a pitch, I realised something: I had a choice.

I could continue the current path, getting what I had always gotten, or I could change. I decided to change.

I thought: 'Fuck it. I don't care anymore. The next person with the ball is going to get tackled by me. Properly.' I was going to seek contact. Damn the consequences[11]. And so I sought him out, whoever had the ball in that moment in time. I hunted him. His name was Drayton. He wasn't an overly big guy, but he was running around like a headless chicken with too much time and space. Until he got too close to me. I hit him with my shoulder,

_____

[11] On a deeper level, I had to acknowledge who was responsible for me being on that field in that division in the first place. It was, of course, me.

with everything I had, putting him flat on his back. It was such a big hit that the referee stopped play to see if he was okay.

He was fine.

Me, I was even better. I was told to swap jerseys and I played for the Witkouse (fifth XV – named for wearing white socks over the standard navy-blue ones) for the rest of the year. One of the highlights of the season was scoring a try and beating Selborne just hours before the Springboks won the Rugby World Cup. Playing competitive rugby was just the ticket for what I deemed to be the real sport beginning towards the end of the year.

As the rugby season ended, I spent the August holidays training to make the first VIII rowing team. Training, training, training. Running, ergo and weights – high repetitions and often twice a day. The outcome didn't so much matter anymore, the training was just something I had to do. I had to be able to look at myself in the mirror and say that I had given it my all, to try and achieve the (deemed now somewhat improbable) goal of rowing first VIII after rowing third VIII the previous season.

As the rowing season began in late 1995, it came as no surprise that I was not in the first VIII for the first regatta of the season. After all, I had spent the previous season in the third VIII. I was put in the Stroke position of the second VIII, which was victorious at the Swartkops Regatta in PE. In truth, I was not too concerned as the real racing was always the Buffalo Regatta and SA Champs held in February and March each year. In between the Swartkops Regatta and the Mayor's Plate, there was an ergometer time trial. Bring it on.

A junior member of the current first VIII had literally not changed (or even washed) his 'lucky rowing jocks' since the season began, such was his excitement at being in the crew. Those jocks would not help him in the time trial though. There was no place to hide there. He was off the pace, quite badly, and I would replace him in the first VIII. He would elect to not row for the rest of the season.

I was in! Somehow it all seemed a bit surreal and rushed. Maybe it was because none of it counted… yet. These regattas and this part of the season were basically just prep work.

We were just getting started.

*

We lost the Mayor's Plate Regatta to a strong Leander crew, a good battle over an extended course of 2500 metres. Those extra 500 metres are a long way when going full tilt.

And so came the December/January break. More ergos, more gym work. It was relentless. On one occasion, I was even found lying on the floor in the gym next to the leg-press machine, having blacked out after a particularly punishing set.

It was also about to get more intense.

I had become friends with the second VIII rowing coach. He was another legend of the South African rowing world, having gone to Junior World Champs twice and stroked the Rhodes Men's A VIII to Boat Race victory in his first year out of school. His name was Andy.

During one of my very rare evening escapades over that December holidays, I went to the Bathurst Ox Braai[12]. Although most years there was 'no thirst like Bathurst', I was very focused on rowing that year. I bumped into Andy and we had a quick chat. As we were concluding our conversation and Andy was walking off, I called out to him: 'Hey Andy, I've been training

---

[12] The Bathurst Ox braai is held annually between Christmas and New Year's Eve at the Bathurst Agricultural Showgrounds. It is a big party where thousands gather and stay overnight in their cars. A braai is meat prepared with an open flame, as opposed to a barbeque, which is prepared with gas.

really hard to make the first VIII.'

Andy stopped in his tracks, swung a look over his shoulder like the hunchback of Notre Dame and said, 'What did you just say?'

'I've been training really hard to make the first VIII!' I repeated, more enthusiastically this time.

With eyes like laser beans and a scowl from hell, he said these words to me before walking off into the crowd of people: 'You don't train to make first VIIIs. You train to fucking win it.'

What? And there it was. There was the step change. This had gone beyond the egotistical, point-proving aspirations of making the first VIII to a whole new level – one of high performance. It was a few weeks before January Camp. Time to lift again. Was this crazy? 'Train to fucking win it'? I wasn't even in the crew yet! It took me a little while to process those words but very shortly after that, I did start training to win it. Time trials and training overall just became more brutal as prep for the January camp continued. This meant regularly dragging my brother or Watty (a member of the previous season's SA Championship-winning crew and National Representative) along to the gym for the ride.

January Rowing Camp was fast approaching[13].

---

[13] For those of you not interested in schoolboy rowing, please feel free to skip to Chapter Four – Early University. There is no need to waste anyone's time here. To summarise, the rowing season was very successful.

CHAPTER THREE

SIX WEEKS IN 1996

Who was this guy, and why was he here? It was January Rowing Camp, 1996. His name was Justin. He was from St Stithians (Saints) in Johannesburg and had come to do Post Matric and row at College. He had rowed in the second VIII in his final year at Saints and was 6'2" tall.

And he was good…

Brother Richard would also attend Rowing Camp (rowing in the U16 A VIII) and complete the final three years of schooling at College. It was one of Dad's proudest achievements to have both his sons attend College.

As we settled into camp life, the two open VIIIs would run/walk the few kilometres from the cabanas where we were staying to the river. This trip soon became a race between the two testosterone junkies of Justin and me as we sized each other out. Because shoes would get wet in the boat, or stolen from the side of the river, this twice-daily journey would also be barefoot.

As far as potential opposition for seats in the first VIII boat, there was also Pete to be concerned about. He had also arrived fit and driven as we stroked opposing boats for the first few days while the coaches observed us from the pontoons. I say concerned, but I was now focused on the bigger picture. 'Train to fucking win it.'

Here is the thing though: I really wasn't that good. But I tried. The finish of my stroke was terrible and the coaches were looking to get that right. On about the fourth morning session – at Rabbit Rocks, 6.6 kilometres up the river – it happened: Andy saw it and screamed approval from 100 metres away as the coaching boat went through the channel and the rowing boat went over the sandbank before the Men's Boat Race start on the way up to the Mill. And wow, did it feel good! The rest of the camp flew by with the usual callouses and boogie boarding in between sessions. I was in the crew with no cause for celebration yet as the job was still to be done. Justin made it too.

Richard's first day at College, and the start of my last year – January 1996.
Dad would pass away in a car accident a little more than two years later.

We also gained our crew song: *Bullet with Butterfly Wings* by the Smashing Pumpkins. Apart from the classic opening line of 'the world is a vampire', the chorus of 'despite all my rage I'm still just a rat in a cage' was just the tonic for the crew when getting ready to race.

The first VIII crew after the January Camp (nickname in brackets, based mostly on surnames) was:

1. Rob (Norm)
2. Justin (Raptor)
3. Brett (Boss)
4. Grant (Poppy)
5. Richard (Watty)
6. Ryan (Donkey)
7. Nick (Hairy Carcass)
8. Mark (Bass)

Cox: Rowan (Heavy D)

The 1996 first VIII was not expected to amount to much. The previous year's crew had won SA Champs for the first time and had an unbeaten season. The average height of that crew was 6'4" and five crew members went on to row for South Africa that year.

To be honest, we never wanted to be like the 1995 crew. Although three members of that crew remained in 1996, we were a new crew with our own qualities. We could not allow the successes of the previous year's crew adversely impact our performance. That said, the preparation the 1995 crew applied for the season would be replicated in 1996. This included attending the Riviera Vaal Regatta in Johannesburg early in the season and going up again to acclimatise to the altitude one week before SA Champs.

So, shortly after camp the 1996 first VIII took a Friday off school and drove the 1000 kilometres or so to Roodeplaat Dam to take part in the Riviera Vaal. In an interesting twist of fate, it was held where SA Champs would be held later that year as the water level was too low at the original venue.

The head-to-head knock-out racing format, however, remained the same. Racing at altitude in a borrowed boat one day after arriving was always going to be a struggle, and we lost to the eventual winners Saints in a relatively close race. As an exercise, it was invaluable as we got to see the famed Joburg crews and appreciate how much work was needed to be successful at the big regattas later in the year, the Buffalo Regatta (virtually our home regatta, held in East London) and SA Champs.

It was a long drive back to Grahamstown on the Sunday afternoon for school on Monday.

The next regatta for us was Border (State) Champs, held outside Stutterheim at Wriggleswade Dam in nothing short of atrocious conditions. Conditions deteriorated so badly during the day that all the races were shortened to around 500 metres, as opposed to the standard 2000 metres.

We failed to execute our strategy properly and lost to Selborne, causing concern for our supporters but probably hardening our resolve that we were a 2000 metre crew. Part of the fall-out of that weekend was an ergo time trial the following Tuesday. We only found out about it mid-way through the day. By this time, I had done so many ergo time trials that it was great to do one with the crew. Nick and I had also been running 'A-Blocks' most nights after evening prayer. The A-Block was a horrible triangle-shaped course that went from the St Andrew's Chapel straight up Cradock Road around St Andrews Prep, left back down the hill on Graham Street and then left again down the home straight past the Diocesan School for Girls (DSG) along Worcester Street. It was a seven-odd-minute running race against each other and a great way to keep the legs moving and the mind sharp. There was no room to slack off. It was hard work straight up the hill, hard around Prep and down the hill, and then harder on the home straight past DSG.

The results of the Tuesday time trial would lead to the dropping of Brett for Ryan (Snoekie). Ryan was a fellow third VIII member from the previous season, who had joined rowing even later than me. He would take up the Number Three position, adding a few more watts to the boat. The crew would remain as such for the final three regattas of the season, being the Selborne Sprints, Buffalo Regatta and SA Champs.

The Buffalo Regatta was the largest regatta on the South African rowing calendar, with schools, universities and open clubs attending. Due to the sheer volume of boats on the water at any one time, participants could only enter two races over the weekend.

Additionally, with a creek entering the Buffalo River with about 700 metres to the finish line, the course was limited to four lanes over 2000 metres as opposed to the usual six. This meant knock-out heats, with the top four fastest times going through into the A final. We drew Saints for our Thursday morning heat and I am quite comfortable stating that we as a crew would rather have died than let them beat us that morning. We may have jumped the start but finished a few lengths up on them and qualified with the fastest heat time. It was little cause for celebration as the real race was on Saturday, but it did give the crew a huge confidence boost.

The Selborne Sprints Regatta is held on the Friday afternoon in between the Buffalo Regatta heats (held on Thursday afternoon and Friday morning) and Buffalo Regatta finals on the Saturday. It was a schools-only regatta with all races being held over 500 metres. Maybe it was because we didn't care for it and had an exceptional 500 metre race plan that we did so well, but the College VIII won it, a year after the 1995 crew had done the same!

We drew lane one and executed the plan to perfection. Quite incredibly, the first IV won as well, with the second IV losing by a bow ball[14] to Saints. The weekend was turning out nicely but 500 metre racing is far more of a lottery than the Olympic distance of 2000 metre racing. The real test would come on Saturday.

And so it came to pass: Saturday 17 February 1996. Our crew would have two races that day, in the IVs around mid-morning/mid-day and the VIII in the early evening in the second last race of the weekend. I'm not sure what emotions I had at the time, save for a real focus on the VIIIs race. Focused, driven, passionate perhaps? It didn't matter; we would have the IVs race first in any event before the big one.

Raptor would stroke the second IV with Snoekie at three, me at two and Norm in the bow seat. The IVs were of absolutely no concern to us. We had perhaps one session as an IV prior to the Buffalo weekend. It could have been the fact that we had lost the 500 metre sprints by a bow ball the day before, or it was hot, or we were nervous, or who knows, but up at the start Raptor and Norm got into a shouting match, with Norm wanting to climb down the boat, or even swim to the stern, to bash Raptor. Nothing like a bit of pre-race tension. We ended up winning the race and tapering towards the end to conserve energy as there were bigger fish to fry. Due to the tight racing schedule, we climbed out of the boat with the first IV climbing straight in it for their race, which they also won. All well and good but we wanted the VIII.

As the hour grew closer, the tide turned, the wind dropped and the anticipation grew. The sun had long moved past the Buffalo River valley and was setting behind the high hills to the west. The first VIII final would be contested between College, St Stithians, Jeppe and KES. Jeppe and KES had rowed significantly slower

---

[14] A bow ball is a small soft ball no smaller than four centimetres that is placed on the bow of the boat. It is used for safety and sometimes to decide very close races.

heat times though, so this was expected to be a two-horse race between College and Saints.

Warren, our coach and master strategist, had us divide the race up into four blocks of 500 metres, with specific things to think about/emphasise during those blocks. The most important of these blocks was the third 500 metres. This was where all crews were taking the most strain and where we would be mentally harder and make our move. Warren had coached last year's Championship winning crew and was an old Saints boy himself. He had also rowed at school under the current St Stithians coach, Paul (himself an old Andrean) – talk about a small rowing fraternity.

We anticipated being slow out of the start but backed our rhythm to beat most crews over 2000 metres. It was just a case of hanging on until they cracked. We also anticipated that at around 700 metres to go (at the creek), Saints would do a push. When they did theirs, we would just squeeze and as they finished theirs, we would do our push, with a bit more length. To ensure a quicker and on-time start, stakeboats had been installed at the 2000 metre mark. This was serious stuff!

With a light tailwind and an outgoing tide, we were in lane three, St Stithians lane four and KES and JEPPE in lanes one and two. As we got under starters orders, the unthinkable happened… Saints jumped the start.

It was bad. Once the crews are lined up, the normal rowing starting protocol is for the umpire to call 'attention' while holding a flag up, pause and then 'row' whilst dropping the flag. However, the word 'row' had not even been uttered and Saints were off. It was so bad our whole crew sat and waited for the race to be re-started, which did not happen. We were late off the start, last even – it was a joke. A sick joke but a joke nonetheless. We had smashed those pricks in the heats and now they had jumped the start, trying to get us. Off we went, trying to catch up. We knew we would have been slow off the start anyway – we had been all season – but now we were behind, behind badly.

No matter, we had four 500 metre pieces to get through. As we got through our start and settled, we looked for a rhythm to get us back in the mix. And rhythm was what Bass and Nick did well...

But Saints kept moving, kept moving ahead. Fuck them, fucking cheaters. I'll admit, I looked out at the boat and saw they had clear water on us at the 1000 metre mark. Still, we held the dogged rhythm.

We began to claw our way back into the race past the creek with 700 metres to go, deep in the killing fields of the third 500 metres, where everyone was taking the most strain and we would be the hardest. And then Heavy D (our cox) said it: 'Number four – look out the boat... now GO!'

I looked to my right and saw George, the Saints' cox. We were half a length down with less than 700 metres to go. Norm screamed 'let's go!' from the bow seat of the boat and everyone in our crew lifted. Ten massive strokes later and we had finally drawn level with less than 500 metres left of the race. The pain was indescribable and the world was becoming a blur. We had pulled the bastards back but there was no time to reflect. We had to lift for home now. The race was not done.

And push we did. Bass and Nick lifted again, and I'd like to say I was present but it was all just pain. We beat them, by clear water, and I was fucked. An unwritten rule in rowing is not to collapse backwards after a race. Forward over the blade (oar) by all means, but not backwards. I lay there, flat on my back, completely broken afterwards, with Snoekie in the Number Three seat congratulating me and Watty in the Number Five seat telling me to sit up.

We had made history. St Andrew's College won the Buffalo

Regatta in back-to-back years, and we as a crew had lost just one of the six races we entered that weekend over the two regattas. We had been staying as a crew at Watty's parents' house and back-to-back victories were a great occasion to celebrate despite provincial (state) trials the following day. These celebrations included a trip to Numbers Dance Club and a very late night/ early morning. No one in the crew really cared for the trials. We were celebrating what (for us) was an astonishing come-from-behind win and an incredibly successful weekend.

Sunday morning and provincial trials rolled around. Everyone was frail and tired. Bass was so frail that I was concerned that he would not be able to row, especially when he could not turn on the taps down at the river to get some water.

As Grey High School (from PE) had performed so poorly at the regattas, they were never going to be in the mix for provincial selection. The Border Crew would be made up of members of the College and Selborne first VIIIs.

The trial consisted of two composite VIIIs rowing up and down the Buffalo Regatta for a few laps and the initial Border boat was made up of the two first IVs from each school, with Norm being swopped into the bow seat after a few kilometres. I did not feel like I was rowing well that day but late in the session I was swapped into the Border boat for a member of the Selborne first IV. Apparently, the boat moved a lot better with me in that seat and so I was selected to row for Border at the Interprovincial Champs, held after the SA Champs at Roodeplaat.

From third VIII one season to provincial colours the next... it was a fairy tale.

Two members of the College crew did not make the Border Crew that year: Raptor and Snoekie.

I remain sorry for both. While I accept the rationale of both the coaches in the selection process (which was to select the best oarsman out of sixteen), I think that the performances over the weekend justified the whole College crew being Border representatives. College won five out of six races and Selborne did not even qualify for the first VIII final of the Buffalo Regatta. I cannot deny being very chuffed at having made the Border VIII, tempered with a certain amount of indifference. The job was not yet done. As Andy had said: 'You don't train to make first VIIIs, you train to win it.'

That job was in a fortnight's time at Roodeplaat. That is where we would meet our destiny. Winning Buffalo meant nothing if we didn't win SA Champs.

*

After spending two weeks back at school, we departed Grahamstown on the weekend of 24–25 February 1996 and travelled up to Pretoria a week before SA Champs. Roodeplaat Dam itself is about half an hour's drive northeast of Pretoria and over 1200 metres above sea level. The air is dry and thin up there. The dam itself is in a nature reserve and animals including zebra, various buck and black-backed jackals can be seen when driving in. It also has occasional issues with the invasive water hyacinth. Frequently called the world's worst aquatic weed, this pest ensures the water remains a varying degree of green, particularly in the shallows, and requires ongoing management. A green film of algae remains on the boat and the blades after each rowing session, which needs to be washed off with fresh water.

Our arrival brought with it illness. What was a sniffle for most was pretty bad for Justin in particular, who was replaced by the legend Andy Mac for a few sessions during the week leading up to the regatta. Andy had also rowed for Rhodes and South Africa and won Silver Sculls and the Grand Challenge. He showed us how to do a racing start, that's for sure! Saturday 2 March was coming.

With one weekend between Buffalo Regatta and SA Champs and a 1000 kilometre-plus journey, there was not going to be time to make many changes as a crew. However, what had been dogging us the whole season was our slow starts. Our rhythm would get us back in any race but our race starts put us behind from the get-go every time. So, we worked on those first five strokes or so. That and course visualisation, including looking out the boat to get a feel of where we were on the course. I was advised to tap off the pressure at the start to eighty per cent as I was washing out Donkey in the six-seat. Increasing the control slightly made us more efficient out of the blocks.

Despite resting for a few days and seeing a doctor, Raptor and Snoekie were still not in good shape as Saturday grew closer. Decisions needed to be made in terms of which races would be rowed and as the VIII was one of the last races of the day, it was decided that the second IV would be scratched from the race. This was quite a pity as we had just won the Buffalo Regatta two weeks earlier. However, it was not worth risking racing ill crew members twice. The bigger prize was the VIII. The first IVs rowed around mid-day, had an amazing race, and won first IVs for the first time in College history. It was a very demanding race and I had some concerns that Bass, in particular, would not recover in time to give it one more go in the VIII.

As the hour got closer, Warren pulled us all together and re-emphasised the race plan, which we all knew in our heads anyway. Immediately after the chat, Justin went off and threw up, such was his illness. To his absolute credit, he did so without telling the rest of the crew as it may well have thrown us off. As we walked to get 'hands on' Pegasus (our racing shell), we saw who we viewed as our biggest rivals, Saints, giving each other hugs after their race plan chat. I recall thinking: 'We've got them.

We don't need to hug each other to get through this. We've got them.'

The memories have, of course, faded over the years, but I remember this: we came out of the blocks faster than earlier in the season and were leading by the 500 metres mark. Knowing our rhythm was our strength anyway and leading from the first quarter of the race, we sat on the other crews and didn't stress. Going through the halfway mark at 1000 metres we had three-quarters of a length over our nearest rivals.

As predicted, Saints pushed with around 750 metres to go and we squeezed while they did it. They moved up a bit but after our ten push, we re-established a comfortable lead, with a lot in the tank, should it be required. All too quickly, we were in the last 500 metres, pushing for home, waiting for the challenge that never came.

We won SA Champs!

'You don't train to make first VIIIs, you train to fucking win it!'

I still think of that epic six-week period of my life. For those new crew members, it was unbelievable. The little crew that could.

To add icing to the cake, the Border VIII racing later in the day rowed down the Gauteng crews to win the Interprovincial Regatta as well. The College second VIII also won their race after narrowly losing to Jeppe by a bow ball at the Buffalo Regatta. So ended a very successful day for College Rowing. The first IV was invited to SA trials the next day and we as a crew would celebrate history. The trials went well for the IV, but with Donkey too old, there would need to be a replacement in the IV should training continue. Bass and Watty were shoe-ins for the first XV rugby team that year and so pulled out of SA squad selection a few weeks later.

In a random act of kindness, the Head of Rowing (and Housemaster of Armstrong) sent a message for me to see him one

Saturday morning, about a month after Champs. We had had a fiery relationship and I wondered what I had done/been caught doing now. As I sat in his office that morning waiting, I pondered how much had happened in recent months. Autumn was in full flight and rugby season was slowly kicking off. The seasons were changing. Leaves were beginning to fall in preparation for winter.

The door to his residence opened and in he walked. 'I just want to apologise,' he said.

'For what, sir?' I was feeling really confused.

'Well,' he said, 'if Watty and Bass had decided to row, the selectors would have looked to you to be the fourth member of the IV to represent South Africa at the World Championships in Strathclyde, Scotland. I have no doubt you would have made it. With them now playing rugby instead and Nick having rowed at World Champs last year, unfortunately, you ran out of luck this time.'

'Wow. Well, thank you, sir.'

From third VIII to winning Buffalo and Champs in the first VIII, representing Border, winning inter-provincials to almost going to World Champs. It had been quite a journey.

While the news from the Head of Rowing had been flattering and much appreciated, I now had another challenge on my hands. With my newfound skills in the rowing boat and commitment on the rugby field, I had not applied myself as best I could in the classroom. The net result was that my mid-year results were underwhelming and my grades were not good enough to get into university. After initially being unimpressed with my mid-year academic performance, my parents acknowledged that I merely needed to focus more on the academics now that the rowing season had finished. I applied myself and performed well enough in the final exams to get into university.

A whole new world awaited, but before university there was

Matric Rage (end-of-school celebrations) in Plettenberg Bay to get through and then my first real job. I developed 35mm film at my uncle's photo shop in Port Alfred over the December holidays. While awesome to have gotten a job over that summer, it was with really mixed emotions as I was not aware of any of my school friends having to do any jobs over that period. In fact, it was a bitter pill to swallow. I was on my feet all day and it was summer, with beautiful weather outside and everyone else on holiday. However, Dad was adamant that I work over that period as he did not intend paying for me to get drunk at university the following year. I could do that on my own coin. While that was all well and good and the money was well earned, working six days a week meant that I was not training for the upcoming university rowing camp.

Without a big overarching mother of a rowing goal and being unable to train at the level I thought was required, I was quite anxious about my first season of club rowing.

22nd S. A. SCHOOLS ROWING CHAMPIONSHIP REGATTA

Bringing home Gold. Brothers from another mother.
College won first VIIIs in back to back years.

CHAPTER FOUR

EARLY UNIVERSITY

After such an epic final season of schoolboy rowing, there was only one university I was going to go to – the best rowing university in the country – Rhodes. It was also very convenient that Rhodes was in Grahamstown, where I had spent the previous five years at boarding school, and Richard would be spending at least the next two years finishing high school.

In early January 1997, I arrived at the Rhodes University Rowing Club (RURC) Camp in Port Alfred. I had not even been accepted into the university yet. Nevertheless, there I was, piling on the kilometres up and down the Kowie River. Five members of the College VIII that won the SA Junior Champs the previous year arrived at the camp. While all the other Rhodes rowers stayed at the Longhursts' (a run-down and perfectly practical large home for student rowers), we stayed at Raptor's house on the Marina. I would be the only one of the five not to row in the Rhodes A VIII during the sprint race season, although I did end up rowing in a very competitive C IV for most of it.

On a broader university note, I was accepted into the Bachelor of Business Science course. This was the source of some pride, particularly for Dad and me as it was not merely a Bachelor of Commerce, it was apparently one better. Socially though, it was a strange few months. The older rowers advised that Orientation or 'O' Week where we would meet other first-year students was a waste of time and we would be better off training on the Kowie. While that may have been true from a rowing perspective, when I did register and move into Jan Smuts Residence for the start of the first term, all the new first-year students thought I was in second year and all the second-year students didn't give a shit what year I was in. I felt I was on the back foot in Jan Smuts from the beginning of my university career.

After Rowing Camp finished in early February, it was up to Grahamstown for university registration and my first RURC toga party. After spending the whole day registering for my courses and missing lunch in that process, I also missed dinner, walking the few kilometres to get to the toga party share house (digs) at a reasonable time. When I eventually got there, I was seriously hungry. Dad had stated expressly that I should not ask anyone staying in digs for any food as they would be hard up surviving in a communal house. I was in a quandary.

I arrived there late and out of what felt like desperation asked Bruce (one of the older rowers) apologetically if I could have any food. Bruce was extremely accommodating, stating with a big smile on his face that he had this 'kiff (very nice) chocolate cake' that he was happy to share.

Chocolate cake? This was awesome! What did my dad know about shared accommodation living? These guys were living like kings! So there I was, eating chocolate cake, so hungry that I was literally picking up the crumbs off the bottom of the tray. I was so hungry and so happy to be getting some food! Then it was goon juice time... who knows what was actually in those tubs of fruit, mixer and alcohol. Whatever it was, it was potent.

While enjoying the goon juice with a belly full of yummy cake,

I noticed Mike sitting in the outside shed. He had been sitting in the same spot all night, barely moving, eyes like piss holes in the snow, just admiring all the sheet-clad ladies wandering around. He had a great vantage point and was going nowhere. I thought, *Wow, he is chilled.*

Then Mike shouted to Bruce: 'Hey, Bruce-o, do you have any more of that kiff chocolate cake, bru?'

NO! I thought. *I have just unintentionally consumed a whole lot of 'magic' cake, including literally the crumbs.* On reflection, the crumbs did look strange and the density of the cake was unusual...

Welcome to Rhodes rowing, where we row hard and play harder!

The club rowing season is long. At school, it had been all wrapped up by early March. At a senior level, it was late April. This meant Easter Camp. For the first time ever, it was held at Wriggleswade Dam outside Stutterheim. The weather was horrendous the whole long weekend and by the end of it, my back had had enough. I dropped out of the last few races of the sprint race season. The Rhodes Men's VIII went on to win SA Champs that year too, against a very good Old Eds crew, making it a great season for Rhodes. The early season camp and Easter camp certainly paid dividends.

*

After a few short months off, which included mid-year exams, it was back to rowing season... for Boat Race. Now, this was a different kettle of fish altogether. Modelled on the Oxford/Cambridge Boat Race, all universities from South Africa are invited. This was a 6.6 kilometre race on the Kowie River from Rabbit Rocks to the fishing jetty. Heats are held on the Thursday for all crews. Based on the result from the previous year, crews in each division start approximately thirty seconds apart and race against the clock. How quickly each crew completes the course dictates whether they race for first and second place, third and fourth place, and so on, in a head-to-head race on the Friday or Saturday.

As a result, the heats were a truly tough event as you had to row your absolute guts out just to see if you were good enough to race in the first and second final. What a great racing format! What a way to train!

The intense focus on one event really appealed to me. The date was clear and the history well-known in the club. Rhodes Men's A VIII had not lost a Boat Race in years. The Men's B VIII had lost the previous year to what was technically an A VIII (the university club that beat them did not have a B VIII). There was certainly incentive and motivation to do well from an overall club perspective.

However, my spine did not cooperate early in the training and as a result, I attended Rhodes East London campus for three weeks of chiropractic work. Upon return, I had weekly intense physio with a student at the HKE (Human Kinetics and Ergonomics) Department and stretched religiously before each rowing session. That really helped and I was raring to go!

During the September university holiday break, we raced. Before... we trained. During regular double sessions, the sense of focus was palpable. We even had an overseas-based 'finishing coach' (Richard) arrive a few weeks before the race – wow, a finishing coach, what does that even mean?

Rich's arrival was eagerly anticipated and one of the first things he did was cut the Dreissigacker oars shorter. What? Cut them shorter, that's a sin!

With Rich on board and the work all done, it was time to

perform. The Thursday heats saw the Men's B crew start in first place and extend that position by over a minute over the course in very windy weather. The A crew and both the women's crews would also win their heats against the clock. This meant that all Rhodes crews would be racing in the first and second-place finals on the Saturday. A good day for Rhodes rowing.

Saturday arrived and Rich provided some calming words and then taped the riggers to reduce the water expected to fill the boat from the winds. Off we rowed around mid-day to Rabbit Rocks to race against (University of Natal) Pietermaritzburg. We rowed well out of the blocks and apart from our number four catching a crab on the home straight, we were never really challenged. While the crew was happy with the result, I wasn't. I had wanted to race, a challenge, meaningful opposition. This result, in my mind, was a fizzer. For whatever reason, the flogging we provided to the opposition was not enough.

It turned out to be a great day for Rhodes, with all four crews winning their A final. Four out of four!

Crew commence drinking beers pretty much straight after each final is rowed so by the time the formal dinner was held at the Port Alfred Town Hall, there were hundreds of athletes who were feeling more than a little mellow. A food fight ensued, much to the disappointment of the dignitaries and it would be the last time the formal dinner would be held on the Saturday night of the event. Organisers moved it to the Thursday night for future years in a successful attempt to improve behaviour. It is far easier to control athletes' behaviour prior to finals racing as opposed to afterwards.

It would also be the last time the Boat Races would be held during the September holidays, due to what could diplomatically be described as disappointing behaviour by various crew members as well as the general students across Port

Alfred that Saturday. Over 500 glasses were broken and various tables thrown into the Kowie River at the local pub – Barnacles. Motorboats were 'borrowed' without the consent of the owners and driven up and down the river. One student even 'took a rest' on the bowling green… during the middle of a game!

I vaguely remember sitting in a fishpond that afternoon, waiting for the Men's A VIII to round the corner from the Bay of Biscay and onto the home straight. Post Boat Race celebrations continued for at least another week. This was hard for me as I didn't feel I had much to celebrate. The race wasn't that hard, so why the excessive celebrations? I didn't get it.

Regardless, I partook (partially) but mostly looked ahead. I had applied to be a student tutor (Stooge) at College and the interviews were held during the week after the Boat Races. Approximately 300 students applied, with perhaps fifteen to twenty interviewed. As an old Andrean, I hoped to be an easy choice; however, some of the other old Andreans didn't even get an interview. With my recently shaved bald head (I wisely removed the racing Mohawk hairstyle on show during Boat Races) charm and wit, I was in![15]

Landing the student tutor role was a saving of about fifty per cent of my total university fees, so my parents were very happy. It felt good to be able to contribute back in some way after all the sacrifices they had made for me to attend College.

As the end of my first year out of school approached, I felt satisfied that the year had been productive. I did change degrees from a Bachelor of Business Science to a Bachelor of Commerce though. Both Dad and I accepted that the maths requirements in the business science course were a bit too challenging for me. There was, however, a surprise in the year-end results… a dreaded summer

---

[15] The Interview Panel included a young Deputy Headmaster, Tom Hamilton, who became Headmaster in 2023.

school for Accounting 102. I had gone into the exam brimming with confidence that I only needed twenty-nine per cent as I had significantly overachieved in the first semester with a seventy-one per cent for the Accounting 101 course. Walking into the exam, I discussed my lack of concern with another student who stated emphatically that both the Accounting 101 and Accounting 102 courses had to be passed independently of each other! This was devastating news and threw me off the exam.

Summer school meant three full weeks in January working office hours in Grahamstown – in preparation for the supplementary exam. This meant no January Rowing Camp in Port Alfred for the first time in years. 1998 certainly started differently.

Nevertheless, I had to acknowledge that my primary responsibility at university was to actually get a degree, not to row. The student tutor role also brought with it additional responsibility – I was to coach the U14s at the rowing camp in late January. That meant daily trips to Port Alfred to coach, or to Grahamstown to attend summer school depending on where I slept that night. Not the easiest.

However, another (and positive) outcome of landing that student tutor role was a car – a VW Golf that my parents bought me. I was so chuffed! I had spent my first year walking around the Rhodes campus and getting lifts from others home to East London. Now I was truly independent and mobile!

I managed to scrape through the Accounting 102 supplementary exam, and summer school, in what would become a regular occurrence for me in coming years. Missing the January Rowing Camp was significant for me, and I was more than a little jealous at the Buffalo Regatta in the middle of February when the Rhodes Crew unexpectedly won the Men's A VIII race.

In what was a very big decision, I decided to take a break from rowing (about the only thing I felt good at) and try something else. I would play rugby for a bit. Just for the sprint race season. With the new coaching role, stooging and working as a barman at the Rat & Parrot, I also needed to find time to study somewhere.

Things weren't all serious though, as I was now mobile in my blue VW with 1800cc of pure power, no power steering and a moody air con. One night, I arrived late to a cross-dressing party in Milner Street. Stooging duties earlier in the evening dictated a late start to the mid-week shenanigans. In a sleeveless summer dress (I got to show off the guns), with a safety pin pinning my dress up high to my quads, a pair of long white socks and sneakers and a blonde wig, I was rocking it. Later in the evening, I wound up at another house with a friend, Angie. We decided to go to get pizza at what could only be described as ridiculous-o'clock.

Driving to the pizza place, we approached the intersection of Beaufort Street heading towards the Cathedral. The robots (traffic lights, for those outside of SA) were very green for me and so I was not paying too much attention. Heading down the hill, I noticed (very late) a green VW golf going far too fast approaching from my left. I slammed on the brakes but was too late to avoid an accident and hit the car in the back right-hand door. I screamed 'no, no, no' as I saw the smoke billowing from the crumpled-up bonnet. I checked on Angie, who was saying that her knees were sore, and then exited the vehicle.

If we had arrived mere seconds earlier, Angie would have been in big, big trouble as the other vehicle would have t-boned into her side of the car. A few seconds later and both parties would have carried on with their lives none the wiser.

Fortunately, the manager of the local restaurant (the Spur) was walking home and witnessed the whole event. Unfortunately, I was in a dress in the early hours of a Thursday morning with the police soon to arrive. Unsurprisingly, I also did not have my driver's licence or any form of identification on me. The cops ended up driving me back to College to get documentation and then drove me to the police station to lodge the details of the accident.

I hadn't had the car for three months and now it was in the panel beaters. I also had to call my parents and explain what had happened. I managed to get a laugh out of them by explaining that although I had been in an accident, everyone was okay, and while I was wearing a dress, at least I didn't have any make-up on as I was running late for the party.

Unfortunately, this would not be my last car accident for the year.

I had lost my independence after having just started enjoying the mobility that a car provides. However, I was okay and focused on the biggest musical event to come to SA in years – U2! I was initially a little indifferent to attending the Joburg concert for a couple of reasons, including the travel required and the sheer cost of the tickets. Now, I also didn't have a vehicle to get me there.

After mulling about it for a few weeks, the folks encouraged me to head up when a ticket became available. My good friend Andy had a ticket to the Golden Circle for a crazy R500 (AUD100), an obscene amount at the time. I would stay at his house, having landed a lift to Joburg with the return trip to be confirmed amongst the Rhodents at the concert – not a problem.

Arriving at the Joburg stadium that hot autumn Saturday afternoon in March 1998 was quite something. Just as I was about to look for mates, I heard my name being yelled from across the crowd – it was Fran, a good friend of mine from school. He ushered me over and showed me a cooler box/chilly bin/esky full of alcohol – the remnants to just be left at the entrance when we entered the concert venue. Drink up, or it all goes to waste. We drank up…

U2 delivered and I thoroughly enjoyed the concert. What I didn't manage to do was arrange a lift back to Grahamstown on the Sunday morning. This was a problem as there was an economics test on the Tuesday night.

Multiple calls to various friends confirmed I had missed the boat (or car in this case). There was no train to Grahamstown that would get me home in time and I had a total of R140 (AUD28) to my name. Now I had done it. I had really messed up.

In my hungover state, I remembered Uncle Al, who worked at South African Airways. Maybe, just maybe, I could fly to Port Elizabeth or East London and hitchhike to Grahamstown in time for the economics test? I really didn't want to hassle my folks with this inconvenience. I called Al and he asked how soon I could get to the airport. He booked me on a plane to PE. Upon arrival in PE, I headed to the help desk, made a friend with a car and jagged a lift to Grahamstown. What an adventure!

What was not an adventure was my performance at university, which was not going well. While I was now playing rugby for the U21 team and enjoying the change, I knew I needed to apply myself to the academic side of university life shortly or risk failing multiple courses.

With the Easter holiday fast approaching and no rowing camps in sight, it was the perfect opportunity to enjoy the next few weeks and then really knuckle down after the holiday and apply myself in the second term, prior to the mid-year exams.

Richard had made a fantastic start to 1998. He was appointed head prefect of Graham House, achieved Academic Colours and was in the First IV, which won the gold medal at the SA Schools Rowing Champs, being re-awarded Rowing Colours in the process. Now he was playing First XV rugby for College and the team was playing in the annual St Stithians Easter Rugby Festival in Johannesburg. The festival dates coincided with the start of the month-long College break between terms, and the Rhodes Easter holiday.

My parents could have flown up to Johannesburg to watch Richard at the festival but opted instead to pick me up in Grahamstown on the Thursday evening before Good Friday and drive up. We would stop halfway up to Joburg, resting the night with friends in Kroonstad. At the end of the festival, all four of us would then travel back to East London to enjoy the rest of the Easter holiday. Dad had bought a second-hand E-Class Mercedes Benz about eighteen months earlier, registration number BBD 567 EC[16] (the EC being for Eastern Cape). On a cloudless night under a big African sky, he gave the car a good workout on the way up to Kroonstad, reaching speeds in excess of 180kph. This was very unusual for him to do.

---

[16] This will become important later.

CHAPTER FIVE

TRAUMA TWO – CAR CRASH

We arrived in Johannesburg on Good Friday and I spent the Easter weekend catching up with old College mates, reminiscing on those boarding school days and watching great schoolboy rugby.

The College rugby team of 1998 was very good, and they certainly benefitted from having three members of the First IV rowing crew in the forwards, being Johnnie, Doug and Rich. They won all three games at the St Stithians tournament and it was the first time in my life that I could remember that everything was perfect. Dad had recently been promoted and was finally earning money commensurate to the value he added to the company he worked for. Mum had been having a lot of issues at work, which had all been resolved. Richard was Head of Graham House, a SA Rowing Champion and a First XV rugby player. Me – I had 'broken up' with rowing and not had any contact with Karen, an on-again off-again flame from school days. I was enjoying rugby, being a barman at the Rat and just having a bit of fun. Unbeknown to anyone, things were going to change forever in the coming days.

Tuesday 14 April 1998 was the day after Easter Monday. It was also the fiftieth birthday of my dad's best friend – Gordon.

Mum, Dad and Richard picked me up that morning and off we went on the 1000 kilometre-plus trip down to the Eastern Cape and to our home in East London. It was a long drive that would take most of the day.

We stopped again at Kroonstad for a few hours to catch up with the same family friends. I walked to the local music shop and bought Matchbox Twenty's debut album *Yourself or Someone Like You*. I bought the Compact Disc (CD) even though the car we were driving only played cassettes. I had heard the songs *Push* and *3am* on the radio and after listening (albeit briefly) to the opening track of the album in the store, I knew I was onto a winner. These were the days when you had to ask a store employee to play the music you may like through one of a handful of earphone sets in the store.

We departed Kroonstad towards home later that afternoon. Dad had driven all day and Mum did not want to drive. I wanted to help out and take some pressure off him, so I started driving just outside Jamestown, about three hours from home. The sun was setting on a long day in the car and a magical long weekend.

About half an hour into my drive, we approached Penhoek Pass. The sun had since set, and the fog/mist on the way down the pass made visibility poor. I was nineteen, driving a Mercedes Benz E220 – not quite invincible but pretty close.

The last thing I recall was a few small red lights coming out of the fog. I don't specifically recall the horrible sound of the shattering glass and shrieking metal as the Mercedes Benz wrapped around the back end of the truck. I don't recall being dragged for over one hundred metres down the Pass attached to the truck while it came to a stop.

Just black. Nothing.

I remember my mum's voice first. Pleading, desperately pleading. 'Get it off him. Get it off him, please!' And the ever-ticking of the emergency lights of the car. On and off, on and off. A relentless orange repeat, never stopping in the darkness.

My head was so sore. The left side of my face was wet and it was difficult to see out of my left eye. I felt like I had been shot in the back of my mouth and could feel a sharp, chipped front tooth from the shattered windscreen combining with the airbag on impact. I had slumped over the steering wheel and now had the open air of the Eastern Cape sky in front of me where the windscreen was moments ago. I can smell diesel and burnt metal.

I didn't understand what had happened. Was this a nightmare? I looked to my right to see my mum clutching her badly broken left wrist, continuing to beg me to get the vehicle off him. I looked to my left... and there was Dad. The roof of the Mercedes was wrapped around his head. His eyes were closed and his glasses had been pushed aside. The seat may have been pushed down in the impact too. He was motionless and making a strange gargling sound. The A-frame pillar behind his left shoulder, separating the front and rear seats, had been crushed on impact. It's an image that will stay with me forever.

And the orange emergency lights kept ticking. On and off, on and off.

I looked back to Mum who was repeating those words over and over: 'Get it off him. Get it off him, please!' I climbed out of the vehicle. It was cold and dark and visibility was poor.

Where is Richard? Where is Richard? I thought. I heard him moaning in pain about his back and found him. He was out of the vehicle and a short distance away, keeled over with the back pain and clutching his severely broken right wrist.

Right, I thought. *If ever there is a time to be calm, it is now.*

I stumbled out of the driver's seat into the back seat of the shell of the car, put my feet on the roof wrapped around Dad's head and pushed like a leg press would be done in the gym. I pushed as hard as I could in my post-concussion state and could not move it.

I am supposed to be strong! This is the most important time to be strong and I cannot move this fucking piece of metal! I pushed and I pushed and I could not move it.

Outside the vehicle, Richard narrowly missed being hit by a passing vehicle in the mist. Help arrived in the shape of some strangers who drove Rich and me to Queenstown Private Hospital sixty kilometres away while the ambulance and rescue vehicles get to the accident scene to pick up Mum and Dad.

My brain hurt as we continue into Queenstown. I was in the front seat with Richard in the back with what would be confirmed as a compressed spine and a badly broken wrist. Arriving at Queenstown Private Hospital, I walked in first, screaming and shouting that there had been an accident, that my brother was coming in now and that my dad was trapped in the vehicle.

I must have looked like quite a sight, with the left-hand side of my face all bloodied and grazed. Left eye closed, shirt ripped and superficial blood stains on my left shoulder and arm. In the haze of arrival into the brightly lit Emergency Department entrance and trying to process the trauma, I remember a nurse sticking a needle into my arm. Things went black.

I woke in the middle of the night in what was the maternity ward of the hospital. A new life was beginning there, one that had not been planned.

In the darkness, I knew Richard was in a bed to my immediate right and Mum diagonally across from me and opposite Richard. In between the us stood a doctor with an exam pad.

'Where is Dad?! Where is Dad?!' I asked in some sort of a concussion/drug-affected/middle-of-the-night state. Half-pleading, half-fearful of the response.

'He didn't make it,' said the doctor.

Words that I can still hear and brought tears while writing this.

'He didn't make it...'

A primal scream exited my throat and my head hurt like someone was stabbing my brain. It was an indescribable pain. I howled and wept and suddenly I was being held by the doctor. What was happening?

What had I done?

What had I done?

I don't remember getting another needle but I awoke the next morning with Mum shattered, still in a state of shock, almost catatonic, with a cast on her left wrist. Richard was virtually immobile and unable to feel the fingers on his right hand due to the plaster of Paris around his broken wrist. His fingers literally looked like pork sausages about to pop. I could move around perfectly fine and located a nurse to cut the cast, allowing blood to flow appropriately to his hand.

The first morning of the rest of our lives was understandably bleak and the drive from Queenstown home to East London was a sombre affair. Gordon and my Uncle Geoff had driven up to fetch us from the hospital. I remember sitting in the back right-hand seat, looking out to the dry, barren autumn fields on the journey back home. I remember smelling terrible from the previous day's long drive, the dried blood on me and the drugs that had been used to sedate me exiting my pores. What was I going home to?

Arriving into East London, we were taken immediately into St Dominic's Hospital and assessed by Dr Watt, a well-known local doctor and family friend. Both Parkin brothers had rowed at College with his son. Doc had a look at my superficial eye, face and shoulder abrasions and checked me out for a concussion.

Mum and Richard were subsequently booked in for surgery later that day at the East London Private Hospital (ELPH) to fix their broken wrists. My head hurt and my heart was broken.

I was taken to a dentist who capped my chipped tooth. It was another sombre excursion. They knew what had happened. What could be said? After a shower and some clean clothes, I went to ELPH to see Mum and Rich and had a panic attack when I arrived. Mum's cousin Colleen was with me when Mum and Rich were being prepped for surgery. Suddenly it all felt too much and very claustrophobic. Colleen took me outside for a walk around the block and I felt better for the fresh air. While Rich and Mum were operated on, I spent the night at Gordon's house. I had been very good school friends with his son Ross, who was a year older than me. While our friendship had drifted post-school, he was still great support. The Clayton and Parkin families had had regular weekends away at Kleinemonde. Such fun and carefree times, looking back.

The following days are a blur. Mum and Rich were recovering at home post their operations. Both would require pins in their wrists to fix the broken bones and Richard would be bedridden for weeks with his compressed spine. The doctors stated that if he hadn't been so fit and strong, his back would have been broken. Neither would regain full mobility in those wrists, and Mum would require multiple surgeries, including a bone graft from her hip months later in an attempt to fix the damage. Mum had also lost her life partner[17]. Rich and I, our dad.

Me: 'May I have some survivor's guilt, please? Upsize? Well, since you're asking, why not?' – concussion and some superficial cuts.

At home, there were the flowers and food that were constantly

---

[17] Dad's passing in 1998 was preceded by the loss of Mum's dad in 1993 and her mum in 1995. Three significant losses all before the age of forty-five.

being dropped off, alongside my vain/ignorant view to just carry on with life. Ha!

Andy called me later in the week after hearing the news. Through his tears, he stated: 'Don't you ever fucking blame yourself!'

And I had been, and I had been having thoughts of taking myself out. I knew where the key to the gun safe was. I knew where I could do it. The thought of my mum having to clean that up slowed down those plans, but it was Andy's words (orders even) that stopped them entirely. I am forever grateful for these words.

What would that approach have achieved? More heartache for my family? No! I was now the unintended head of the household. I had responsibilities. I had a choice as to how to deal with this going forward.

What was the College motto?

Nec Aspera Terrent – 'difficulties do not dismay us'. Well, I may be dismayed; however, I would still continue.

In the luggage taken from the car that night was my newly purchased Matchbox Twenty CD.

It had been in the footwell behind Dad's seat when we crashed. The CD cover was all cracked but the CD itself was fine. I played the album on the Pioneer Hi-fi in my room. It was one of the last gifts from Dad, who had been working for the group that imported the Pioneer brand into South Africa. It was a six-CD shuffle – high quality at the time!

In the opening bars to *Real World*, Rob Thomas sings: 'I wonder what it's like to be the rainmaker? I wonder what it's like to know that I made the rain…' Wouldn't it be nice to wonder such a thing? I was wondering what had happened to my life and the impact of the damage I had caused.

Track two came and it was *Long Day*. Oh, these past few days had been long, so long. And on to *3am*. Despite having cancer, Rob's mum still tries to look after him. My mum was broken, and she was trying to do the same.

To track four and one of the reasons I bought the album: *Push*. 'She said I don't know if I've ever been good enough, I'm a little bit rusty and I think my head is caving in. And I don't know if I've ever been really loved, by a hand that's touched me and I feel like something's going to give, and I'm a little bit angry.'

This is me.

I listened to it end to end. It was forty-six minutes of musical genius and closed with *Hang*, an acoustic guitar-driven song about a breakup. I had broken up with the innocent Grant. I had broken up our family.

In the coming weeks, I would have dreams of Dad. Dreams of Dad being okay, still alive and well. One dream he was in the driveway.

'You're okay! You're okay!' I said to him ecstatically.

He was smiling and happy.

'Let's go and tell Mum. Let's go inside and tell Mum!'

Dad just smiled and shook his head, and then he walked slowly down the driveway and disappeared.

I had another dream a few weeks later back in Grahamstown. It felt like Dad was going away for good. I woke up and looked at the bedside table. The watch he had been wearing during the accident lay there and it had stopped. You could not make it up.

And in my darkest moment, she came back. My childhood sweetheart. We had been on again and off again for the better part of two years. Karen contacted the Claytons to see if she could visit me. I said yes. She arrived at the house with eyes like saucepans. I recall nothing of the conversation but remember thinking that it took immense courage to contact me when we had not been on speaking terms for months. It is something that

I will always have great respect for her doing. Karen was always there for her friends. That is what I became – her friend.

Somehow, on the Saturday night, both Mum and I attended Gordon's fiftieth birthday party, with Richard bedridden. There was the physical distance we had travelled in the days prior and there was the emotional toll of reconciling what had happened on that Tuesday night, just four days earlier. Best laid plans and all. Gordon toasted missing friends in his speech. The elephant in the room was an understatement. It felt like a woolly mammoth.

Dad's death was followed by a lot of formalities. There was the autopsy[18], the last will and testament, the coroner's report, and police charges to deal with. I had a culpable homicide charge against me due to there being a death on the roads. I had the choice of making a statement to either the police or our lawyers. I chose the lawyers. The charges were dropped, but that would not be the end of the legal wrangling.

And of course, there was the funeral, which was held at the Trinity Methodist Church in Oxford Street, East London. I don't remember which day of the week it was; however, apparently, that day had more attendees than Christmas. The place was packed. Dad had been a member of Round Table and a local businessman for decades.

Due to the unexpected crowds, Mum, Rich and I were chaperoned into the church through a side door before the service started. Uncle Geoff, who had picked us up in Queenstown after that fateful night, spoke on behalf of the family. I saw the closed coffin and didn't think that they really put Dad's body in there for the funeral ceremony. Was Dad now really in a box?

---

[18] The autopsy would reveal that Dad died from one broken rib, which severed his aorta, the main and largest artery in the body. The aorta distributes oxygenated blood to all parts of the body. With it severed, Dad may have experienced a feeling similar to going to sleep. He was forty-seven years old.

Honestly, what has happened?

The coffin was carried out to the hearse by some of Dad's closest friends and we exited the church out the front door. There were rows and rows of people outside and I could hardly see through the tears in my eyes. Everything was blurry and my head hurt so much. I remember seeing Nick, my good old rowing friend, and his parents there. And Gwynn, another old friend from Kingswood and Kleinemonde. Aunty Rita and Uncle Neville, and of course, there was my dad's sister, Aunty Jen. Mum's brothers (Uncle Buster and Uncle Rod) also made it down from Mpumalanga. There were many, many more people in attendance but blurred vision and heightened emotions prevented much more interaction with them. It was just too raw. We were chaperoned back to the car and driven home. A wake was held at the Round Table Clubhouse. Rich, Mum and I did not attend. I certainly could not have handled a drink at that time. My mum's brothers attended on our behalf.

Life simply did not make sense.

CHAPTER SIX

LIFE AFTER DAD

After the formalities of the funeral, we settled into life without Dad. Richard remained bedridden. Mum was not recovering well from the operations required to correct her badly broken wrist and developed an issue with a frozen elbow. My family needed care. I remember shaving Mum's underarms as she could not do it herself, wracked with guilt over what 'I' had caused.

The April university holiday break was ten days, whereas the College break between the Easter and Trinity terms was for a month. With Mum and Rich requiring ongoing support, I did not rush back to Grahamstown when Rhodes re-commenced for term two, opting instead to look after my family. This put me further behind in the studies I was meant to pick up post the Easter break. When College returned and my stooging obligations re-commenced, Rich and I returned to Grahamstown. This left Mum alone in her house for the first time, Rich injured and unable to play for the first XV, and me, three weeks further back in my studies. I had felt pressure before the Easter break; now Dad had passed and the rest of us were dealing with that and the trauma of the car accident. This was unprecedented.

On the recommendation of family and friends, the three of us went to see a psychologist together. I was adamant I did not want to attend. What was talking about it going to change? Psychologists were for crazy people. For weak people even. For those who cannot handle things like a man, on their own[19]. I went to keep Mum happy (what a bizarre thought, given the circumstances) and continued to naïvely think I could just carry on with life.

A few weeks after returning to Rhodes, there was a mid-week U21 rugby game in East London. This required driving back to Grahamstown in the dark afterwards in another student's vehicle. Sitting in the middle of the back seat on the way back to Grahamstown, I thought I saw a dead cow in the middle of the road. I wept uncontrollably for the rest of the trip. Ludumo[20], a fellow Old Andrean held me close the rest of the way. It was then that I realised I needed help. I could try to manage this thing on my own, which was clearly failing and unsustainable, or I could look at other options. I was responsible for getting myself 'right' and I chose to put my ego aside and engage professional help.

I started seeing a psychologist who worked at Rhodes. Mark was a good sounding board. He looked just like how I thought an academic psychologist would look, too: a greying bushy beard and curly hair, slightly portly with glasses and what I considered to be hippie-style clothing. Piles of papers and books all over his desk. More books on over-stacked shelves throughout his office. He was like a real-life version of Robin Williams in *Good Will Hunting*. All I was looking forward to was the next Boat Race season. That was my focus: get through the mid-year exams and then back to 'the only thing I've ever been good at'. That would buy me time and allow me to focus on something positive. 'Whatever gets you

---

[19] There was (and probably remains) a huge stigma for men surrounding psychologists and their craft. Of course, now I realise their value in improving human performance overall, and not just to help during times of adversity.

[20] Ludumo passed in late 2022. RIP brother.

through,' as Mark would say.

As the mid-year exams approached, what I didn't appreciate (or potentially acknowledge) was that apart from being way behind in the curriculum, I was seriously struggling to sit at a desk and study. In fact, I was avoiding sitting at a desk entirely. Images and flashbacks of the accident would come randomly into my head whenever I tried to concentrate on the paper in front of me. I had no idea how to fix it and tried in vain regardless. I failed all but one of the mid-year exams. On a positive note, Richard would make a comeback on the rugby field, playing the last four games of the season for the first XV with a heavily strapped wrist, and be awarded rugby colours.

My second university Boat Race season commenced in July 1998, providing respite from the thoughts in my brain. Concentrating on rowing was very different to sitting at a desk, having car crash images invade your thoughts. My back, though, still did not cooperate and I spent most of the season rowing in a corset. I also swapped to bow-side, which helped reduce the constant dull pain in my lower back. Somehow, I was in the Men's A squad and ended up being the Spare Man that year. Rhodes won four out of four again, winning the Men's A and B VIIIs and Women's A and B VIIIs in what was a real vintage few years. I was an angry man though, unnecessarily hard on my performance in the heats, and despite beating Wits in the final (who were more of a challenge than Maritzburg the year before) I wanted more. I remember looking up as we went under the first bridge on the home straight during the final and seeing what looked like Dad on the bridge, watching. Mum and Dad had watched us row to victory the year before. So much had changed.

After Dad's accident, the only thing I wanted to do was row.
Rhodes won out of four again that year.

Boat Races out of the way, it was time to prep for the end-of-year exams. The struggles with sitting down and trying to concentrate continued. However, at least I managed to get into another summer school, this time for Statistics 101. I finished the year with a dismal academic performance.

I also had the Graham House Supper speech to prepare for. House Supper is attended by the parents of those students leaving College at the end of the year, so Mum and I attended with

Rich. Traditionally, the father of that year's Head of the House gave an address about life after College at this ceremonial event. The address would have been delivered by Dad; however, in the wake of the accident, it became my role. The Housemaster proposed we swap the speeches – with the father of the Deputy Head of House delivering the main address instead, and with me performing a toast of sorts. I agreed.

On the night, I acknowledged Dad's passing in the speech. Richard's speech in response led to a standing ovation from those in attendance.

Life goes on, whether we want it to or not.

*

When I registered back at Rhodes at the beginning of 1999, the Faculty of Commerce advised that I should have been excluded due to the previous year's academic results. I was promptly put on academic probation. That was what I needed, a bit more pressure. Detailing the events of Penhoek Pass and Dad's death to the Faculty fell on deaf ears.

I missed the January Rowing Camp again due to the Statistics 101 summer school, yet was appointed Men's Rowing Club Captain mid-season. I also started dating a girl who would cut herself whenever we had a disagreement. This made for interesting Thursday morning tutorials with her when I knew why she was wearing long sleeves.

I started behaving poorly in March, not being myself. I was short with friends, angry and generally a combative and unhappy man. I went to see Mark who offered the following advice:

1. It was coming up to the one-year anniversary of the accident and this was normal post-trauma behaviour.
2. Just because I had experienced this ridiculously shit event

did not exclude me from experiencing future (potentially) ridiculously shit events. I had not received a 'your life will now be perfect card' as part of the deal. Life simply did not work like that.

I took his advice to heart and experienced the first anniversary. It was terrible, and I was naïve to think it would be anything other than that. April 14th remains easily my toughest day of the year. As a community, we are very good at coming together to support people when a loss occurs. Life then carries on and events like the first Christmas, the first birthday and the first anniversary of a loved one's passing are forgotten. Life goes on for those less impacted. It can stand still on those days for those who lived through it.

I struggled through the mid-year exams and would not be able to row Boat Race competitively, breaking my finger playing in an inter-res rugby match. A pin was required to fix the break, which would regularly get caught on items like bed sheets, pillowslips and clothing. I thought it wise to avoid the gunnel of a rowing boat with a piece of metal literally sticking out of the tip of my finger. The pin was removed a few days before Boat Race, and Rich and I ended up rowing in a scratch Rhodes C VIII. The crew came third in the B VIII heats and finished fourth in the finals. Another testament to the depth of Rhodes rowing at the time. It wasn't a bad performance; although, again, I was hard on myself for not winning the third/fourth final. I had to straighten the finger after each rowing session, which would bend and lock in place around the blade.

Approaching the end of my second year as a student tutor and my third year at university, I wanted a year with friends in a digs for what would be my final year at Rhodes and in Grahamstown. I also wanted to give rowing a full go and just focus on that. It was, after all, the only thing I felt I had ever been good at.

Friends found a place in Milner Street where seven men in their early twenties would live the following year.

Somehow, I avoided academic exclusion from Rhodes and not having to attend summer school. Things looked good for the January 2000 Rowing Camp. What I had forgotten, though, since the years leaving school, was prepping for the camp. The running, weight-training and ergo sessions that are required in preparation before camp even starts. My back simply did not cooperate and I dropped out of the camp in the first week. Heartbroken, I returned to East London and managed to find a chiropractor who, after looking at the MRI scans and x-rays, identified my issue straight away – the facets of my L5 were asymmetrical. This meant one side of my lower back liked to go up and down (vertically – as it should) while the other side did not. Rowing sweep oar (using one oar as opposed to two) loaded the spine each stroke, irritating it, particularly if I rowed on stroke side.

'You're genetically inferior,' the chiropractor said, advising that about ten per cent of the population have the same disposition and are not ever aware of it.

The diagnosis was six months to fix. Okay, no sprint race season; however, we were still good to go for Boat Race in my final year at university – that's good! I threw myself into three-day-a-week gym sessions (the chiropractor did not recommend any more) and even got swimming in the Rhodes pool to keep the cardio up. I was going to do this. I was going to salvage something of my Rhodes rowing career and my first few years out of school.

Of course, unable to row, I needed to maximise the Milner House opportunity. With Orientation Week starting late January, it was time to make it count with a train-hard, drink-harder approach. Living with six other men who were also in their final year meant much deviant behaviour. Rehab training went well and I was quite happy being on my own, having broken up with the girlfriend in late 1999. She, in turn, had dropped out of university. While that may not have been my fault entirely, I was a factor. This did wonders for the guilt… again.

I remained bitter about the accident though, penning this over the second anniversary period:

'Why I'm so bitter…

I'm so bitter because no one has a fucking clue what I've been through.

And I've still got such a long road to travel.

I'm bitter because my eyes have seen too much for a person my age to have seen, because I feel I'm not really compatible to people my age – I know too much about the harsh realities of life.

I'm bleak because no one knows and EVERYONE FORGETS.

They can't compare and they can't relate…

Deep down, I don't think I really want them to.

Because it's been two years and it seems like yesterday.

I can visit the spot anytime in my head.

Rerun it over and over, but make no changes.

Why?'

Drinking hard, training hard and studying a little, I managed to get through the mid-year exams and was totally focused on winning the Men's A VIII Boat Race in September. I even went so far as to borrow an ergo machine from the Rhodes Rowing Club for the July holidays. Unfortunately, once the chiropractor stated I could row again, I started getting referral numbness from my knees down when I sat on the ergo for more than ten minutes. Despite a fair amount of work and being submitted to a significant amount of pain in the chiropractic adjustments, I was going to be a non-starter for Boat Race. I was devastated. This was my identity. I had trained for half a year just to get into a position to have a go. This is just life, Grantie…

Rhodes Men's A VIII would lose Boat Race for the first time in eleven years in 2000. Fortunately, I only watched the heats, driving up to Joburg to watch the Sydney Olympics with Andy, where Don and Ramon (representing South Africa) made the A final in the Men's pair.

Despite not being able to row, I still wanted to remain active. If anything, I knew keeping active was good for me, both physically and mentally. I heard about the Energade Triathlon Series race being held in Port Elizabeth. With no bike or triathlon kit, I entered the sprint race (750 metre swim, 20 kilometre bike and 5 kilometre run) on a whim. I swam in a surfing wetsuit, completed the ride on a borrowed mountain bike with the helmet on back to front and trundled through the run, trying not to let my calves cramp up. It felt good to race again, even if I was so off the pace and out of my comfort zone in a new sport. The Port Elizabeth beachfront would be the setting for a few more triathlons in years to come.

It would also have been Dad's fiftieth birthday on 12 October that year. I wrote this on the day:

'He would've been fifty today…

I would've made a speech at the party

But there is no party and no celebration

Who actually remembers it was his birthday today?

What few actually care?

For the closest, it brings back the agony of the last few minutes with him.

Memories of a horrific accident and unanswered questions

An accident experienced by four, only three of which would survive. Which will never get better, merely be dealt with better.

He would've been fifty today, but one day I'll be able to celebrate him, I swear on it.

Just not yet.'

12/October 2000

He would've been 50 today...
I would've made a speech @ 1 party

But there is no party and no celebration
Who actually remembers it was his birthday today
What few actually care?

For the closest it brings back the agony of the
last few minutes with him.
Memories of a horrific accident and unanswered questions

An accident experienced by four, only 3 of which would survive
Which will never get better, merely be dealt with better

He would've been 50 today, but one day I'll
be able 2 celebrate ~~have~~ him, I ~~sear~~ swear on it.
Just not yet...

Journal entry on what would have been Dad's 50th birthday –
12 October 2000.

Adding to the range of emotions experienced in 2000 was the Supreme Court case that I was summoned to be a witness in. Dad's insurance company was suing the trucking company involved in the accident. The court date was set for late in the year. The insurance company claimed the reason for the accident was the dirt and dust at the back of the truck caused from driving on dirt roads earlier in the day. This, the insurance company claimed, significantly impacted the visibility of the truck's back lights. The truck had been inspected by a College parent the day after the accident, who would also be a witness in the court proceedings.

The court case forced the intentional recalling of the trauma as opposed to the intrusive images I would experience when trying to study. First with our legal team in prepping for the witness stand, and then secondly in the Supreme Court itself during the trial. I was to recount the worst day of my life in the pressure cooker environment of a Supreme Court, just so some insurance companies can settle a score. Lucky Grantie.

With Mum and Richard in attendance, I took the witness stand and after responding to the rehearsed questions from our lawyers, I fielded questions from the defence team. Their approach was to discredit me and create doubt for the court. I was requested to recount the accident again and was then peppered with questions...

- 'Yes, I was concussed during the accident.'
- 'No, I was not aware of the notoriety of Penhoek Pass.'
- 'No, I do not believe I had been driving too fast.'
- 'No, I was not particularly tired at the time. I had sat in the car all day up until that point.'
- 'No, if any other family members had thought I had been driving too fast they would have told me to slow down.'

Final question: 'In the moments immediately after the accident, do you recall your brother screaming: "I told you you were going too fast. I told you!"'

My head hurts. I was flung back into the memory, searching for those words. I didn't remember hearing that. Did Richard say that? Did he warn me moments before impact? Did he scream those words after? I really didn't recall.

'No, I don't recall Richard stating that.'

'No more questions, M'lord,' the defence said as they released the witness. I left the witness box and walked out of the court. On the benches outside, I wept uncontrollably in Mum's lap and asked Richard if he recalled saying that. He denied it. Still, it played on my mind...

Days later, the truck driver was called to the witness box and questioned as to what he heard that night. He was asked specifically what language Richard had used.

'Afrikaans,' replied the truck driver.

The Parkins are an English-speaking family. There was no way Richard would have spoken those words in Afrikaans. The truck driver's credibility was significantly tarnished. While I felt vindicated upon hearing that, it was cold comfort in the shit experience of being involved in the case itself. It would not bring Dad back. This was just about money.

Dad's insurance company won the case.

As the end of the year approached, I felt uneasy about the next chapter of my life. I was going to complete a Bachelor of Commerce in four years, a year later than many. However, Management and Commercial Law were not particularly strong majors and I felt I needed more. I had outgrown Grahamstown, having spent nine years in the beautiful town. It was time for a change... and more studying.

East London had a satellite Rhodes University campus. I decided I would head back to my hometown and commence Economics III there. I hoped this would provide my resume with the necessary substance to enter the job market with confidence.

Karen was also studying there. We had remained friends since Dad's accident and she would regularly call me while I was studying in Grahamstown. In late 2000, on the day she was going overseas with her then-boyfriend, she called advising that the relationship was over. I just knew that we would be getting back together when she returned.

With final semester exams completed, I completed a Bachelor of Commerce degree and took some comfort from not 'wasting' those years at Rhodes.

CHAPTER SEVEN

BACK TO EAST LONDON

In the first two months of arriving back in EL in 2001, I would coach Clarendon Girls School Rowing Club for the season, commence studies at Rhodes East London (RUEL) campus, get back together with Karen and start working for PricewaterhouseCoopers (PwC). I was a busy man.

I would also occasionally take a single scull out and row up and down the Buffalo River. I did not want to row in a crew for fear of letting them down with the moody spine. That did create some inner turmoil as I was asked many times to do so. Sculling, though, was so exhilarating! I couldn't let anyone else down, I could stop rowing if the numb legs and feet got too much. I was free![21]

As the relationship with Karen developed, she began hanging around at the river and eventually rowing herself. A few more RUEL ladies joined and the beginnings of the RUEL Rowing Club were established. I remember walking into the Head of Sports Admin's office one morning, stating that I wanted to start a rowing club, affiliated with Leander, one of the oldest rowing clubs in South Africa and the only active senior club in East

---

[21] I would enter Silver Sculls one year, however, would never reach the same heights as those at College again.

London at the time. It was pitched to be a match made in heaven – athletes from the university and equipment and experience from Leander. RUEL Rowing Club was launched in late 2001.

With a strong recruitment drive, we managed to entice six university ladies and two Clarendon grade twelves to train for the university Boat Race later that year. Finding a cox would prove challenging though. It was no mean feat that we got a crew down to Port Alfred that year and I would get a sobering wake up from a coaching perspective. While the crew improved substantially as a unit in prepping for the race, the horsepower wasn't there.

The crew came sixth out of the nine odd B Crews in the heats. The fifth-placed crew was RAU (Rand Afrikaans University), who finished thirty-two seconds faster in the heats.

Racing in the fifth/sixth final the next day, the fledgling RUEL ladies' crew was on a hiding to nothing. Insurmountable task, I thought. You cannot make up that much time. Then I looked at the crew lists and noted the age of the RAU cox – nineteen. She didn't know the Kowie River like I did. Our cox (also named Grant) did not feel comfortable racing the finals so I (all 85 kilograms at the time) squeezed my rotund rump into the cox[22] seat.

The plan was quite simple. We had to get out fast; otherwise, we were buggered. As the tide was coming in, the fastest water was over the shallow sandbank in front of Riverside Chalets. We would need to get at least half a length up on them and then I was to push the RAU crew deep into the channel by turning our boat towards theirs and into the incoming tide. Theoretically, their cox would not want to clash oars with us, let alone get their boat damaged, and would move across into the deeper water and incoming tide. This would slow down their boat speed

---

[22] The cox (or coxswain) typically weighs 50–55 kilograms – much like a horse jockey – and provides racing instructions to the crew.

significantly, and fame and glory would be ours!

I prepped the ladies that they needed to be super focused and ready at the start. The gun went off and we were racing! The crew gave me half a length by the time we reached the dog-leg (a slight kink in the river) and I shoved the rudder towards stroke side and towards the unsuspecting RAU crew.

'RUEL, move over!' yelled Ramsey the Race Marshall as I intentionally moved towards RAU. I had warned our stroke side to just hold on to their blades and the whole crew to keep their eyes in the boat.

Ramsey yelled again. 'RUEL, move over!'

Whatever, Ramsey... I got this!

I lift my hand in acknowledgement of Ramsey's instructions while driving the RAU crew into the deep water and incoming tide, then shoved the rudder bow side and toward the shallow water. Bye-bye, RAU... smell ya later.

Against the odds, we won. Heaviest cox in Boat Race history for sure, with one of the lightest crews. It was easily one of the most fun rowing victories I would experience. That evening, the RUEL Head of Sports Administration said he'd never seen anything like it in his life. The celebrations were huge and the weekend was soured only by Simone (a crew member) falling off the pier later that night while directing a car into a parking space. A trip to the local hospital led to a few stitches to her head and a set of crutches for an injured ankle. In the following days, Simone would require further cosmetic work to correct the initial stitching, and a broken wrist and ankle were confirmed. It can be dangerous work being a car guard.

At the 2001 RUEL Sports Awards dinner later that year, the newly established Rowing Club won the Performance of the Year award. I would coach the crew the following year when they came third (again beating RAU), racing against the B VIIIs and the

Rowing Club won Club of the Year at the 2002 Sports Awards dinner. I would also commence a Post Graduate Honours Degree in Economics part-time, in an effort to be more employable.

In 2003 the RUEL Women's Crew (in their third Boat Race) raced the other A boats and came sixth. It was a great performance on reflection. I may not have been able to row anymore; however, I could coach all right. Things would change for the worse in 2004 when Karen and I were voted off the Committee of the Rowing Club we had worked so hard to establish. Being essentially kicked out of the club that we helped found hurt. A lot. Once again, I felt as if I had lost my identity and in a sense, I had. I had lots of time on my hands and that was not something that was good for me. I needed another mountain to climb. That mountain would be the 2005 Ironman Triathlon in Port Elizabeth, where I had completed my first sprint-distance triathlon five years earlier. Karen and I entered months before and used a generic Ironman program from a book to train. We would cycle to the other side of King William's Town and back, and to Stutterheim and back as part of the training. Hours upon hours of training. Long and slow. Some may say the perfect remedy for dealing with (or at least delaying dealing with) the heartbreak of the rowing breakup, let alone managing the loss of Dad.

However, Ironman is not your saviour. I would learn this. And need to re-learn this a few more times. While it is not your saviour, it can change your life for the better. Your entire perspective on what you can achieve is permanently changed once you complete one. The distances are just silly: 3.8 kilometre swim, 180 kilometre bike followed by a 42.2 kilometre run, all to be done in under seventeen hours. Ironman race day itself is a special day, a celebration. From the realisation of the hours of effort by the participants, to the sacrifices of their supporters, to racing alongside world champions on the same track as you and at the same time. In what other sport does that happen?

With all the training completed, there is still also the requirement of acceptance. Acceptance that the weather could be foul. That you could have a puncture or even multiple punctures. That you may cramp up. That you may not get your desired finishing time. That you may not finish at all! In that sense, it is a great way to buy anxiety.

Ironman Day in PE in 2005 dawned in spectacular fashion, watching the sun come up over the water in Algoa Bay. After a leisurely 3.8 kilometre swim it was onto to the bike. I remember hearing Raynard Tissink coming before I saw him, one full bike loop ahead of me, a mere 60 kilometres! Raynard was one of the athletes tipped to win the event and he looked every bit of it as he flew past. About six hours later and still on the bike, I would hear the helicopter again and I knew someone quick was approaching. It was someone in a Red Bull tear drop racing helmet, the lead female. Natascha Badmann – the Swiss Miss and five-time world champion. As she came flying past, she looked back, smiled at me and asked if I was having a good race – amazing!

After just over seven hours in the saddle, I peeled myself off the bike and felt euphoric – only 42.2 kilometres left to go! What kind of a mindset is that? After 183.8 kilometres and over eight hours of exercise already completed, 42.2 kilometres wasn't so long anymore. I didn't even care that Raynard was running down the final chute before I'd even started the run leg. He ended up more than 42.2 kilometres ahead of me! *Oh well, next time,* I thought to myself.

I started off the run at what felt like a cracking pace and then saw Karen, who looked like a deer in headlights. I was about fifteen minutes ahead of her and suddenly had thoughts of her not finishing. I even had thoughts of retracing my steps back on the course to ensure she didn't stop. Fatigue can make you crazy. The run turned to a walk as I slowed for her to catch up. While walking through the aid stations, I replenished myself on a concoction of potatoes and raspberry juice… why? I do not know.

Karen caught up to me and it quickly became apparent that running with that combination of food in your stomach was not conducive to feeling good. With the food slushing around, we approached the end of the first (of three) 14 kilometre laps and the finish line area. In front of thousands of spectators, my stomach had enough and decided this was the best time to purge. Hands on my knees, in the middle of the road, I cleaned it out good and proper. Multiple hurls. I could sense people pointing and me not caring at all. A colourful blend of potatoes and raspberry juice all over the asphalt.

The ambulance arrived and the attendant wanted to pull me from the course. I looked at him and can hardly focus. He had a long scar across the side of his face and I wondered where he got it. The whole place was spinning. Karen told him that I'm fine and I just wished his head would stop moving in circles. He let go of my arm and I kept moving as the ambulance drove oh so slowly behind us while we started lap two (another 14 kilometres)…

The cramps started shortly after, mainly in my calves. We ended up running from one lamp post to the next, then walking for the next two lamp posts for over 20 kilometres in wind and rain and darkness. Eventually, we completed the second, and then the third and final 14 kilometre lap, crossing the finishing line just after 10 p.m. where I high-fived Evan, a fellow East London competitor on the way down the finishing chute.

We were Ironmen!

Sense of identity restored, I did not think too much of

becoming an Ironman at the time. Many others did though, and the significance certainly grew in the coming months. I again, in what remained the theme, was hard on myself for not performing better.

*

Hiccup on the rowing aside, things were going well; I completed the Economics Honours Degree at the end of 2003 and continued working at PwC. Karen and I had been together since she returned from Australia and New Zealand at the beginning of 2001. The pressure about what I was going to 'do with my life', though, remained. There were some big questions that I felt still needed to be answered. I was now nervous that an Honours Degree in Economics was not going to 'buy me' the job security I craved. I felt I needed something meatier. That of course was accounting. With Dad being a Chartered Accountant and Mum being a bookkeeper, some may say that it was always my destiny. In 2004, my eighth consecutive year at university, I commenced studying accounting.

The other big 'life' question was where would we live? Where would we spend our days? We had seen East London change over the years and did not see a future there. Crime rates were increasing and municipal service delivery standards dropping. Education and health standards were also declining and the only beach you could go to at night was the one with a 24-hour armed guard. We viewed East London as a microcosm of what would eventually happen to the rest of South Africa. This opinion removed the options of other coastal towns in SA, indeed SA entirely. We felt we had a responsibility to our future selves and the family we were going to create together. So what options were there? Where could we go? The northern hemisphere was too cold – there goes half the world. South America was apparently much the same as SA, so there goes another continent. We literally drew a line across the globe from East London and hit Australia. Perth was apparently full of South Africans, so why would we want to go there? And then there was the east coast of Australia, with places like Sydney (too big), Newcastle (never heard of it) and Brisbane. Isn't that where the Queensland Reds are from?

On the other side of Australia and across the Tasman Sea was New Zealand, which of course was too cold again. And on the other side of New Zealand was South America. Done. Decision made. We were migrating to the east coast of Australia. Such a simple way to make a major life decision.

We had braais, Australia had barbeques. We played cricket, Australia played cricket. We played rugby, Australia played rugby. This would be easy.

It was not. The Australian culture was very different.

The migration process is painful. It requires ongoing commitment to an outcome often years away. It is long. It is expensive. It is invasive. You need to provide supporting documentation for your degrees (which need to be independently assessed), bank account statements and police clearance certificates. It takes time to collate and submit all this. You need to pass an English test. You need support. The time zone difference is frustrating. It can feel as if you know nothing and you can question whether you are doing the right thing.

After almost six months of saving, we had enough money to engage a large South African-based migration company for the princely sum of R15,000 (about AUD3,000 at the time) to help process our visa application. That visa submission itself was another R10,000 (AUD2,000) and necessitated a trip up to Pretoria to complete the Independent English Language Testing

System (IELTS) exam, required as part of the application and another additional expense. The migration agent advised that as teachers were on the skills shortage list; Karen would be the primary applicant. We had our concerns about this approach as part of that requirement was to have a minimum of three years' experience and Karen only had just over two years at the time of submission in early 2005. Not to worry, the agent advised, the visa processing takes well over a year, so by then the relevant experience will have been obtained.

Of course, this was not the case.

In October 2005, we received the 'exciting news' that our application had been accepted and that we could live in regional Queensland or regional South Australia. Our visa would not allow us to work in any state capital for a period of two years. We were devastated. We were highly qualified individuals and now we felt we were being dictated as to where we could live in this new country. It was harder to get roles in regional areas and those roles would certainly pay less too. It felt like Australia wanted us but we would arrive as second-rate citizens. There had to be other options. One was to re-submit a permanent residency application from South Africa and wait another year. Another was to get a job offer, commence working in Australia and re-submit the permanent residency application from there.

Obtaining a job offer was a virtually impossible task to accomplish without being on the ground in Australia. So, ever the driver, one Saturday night I searched the internet for jobs in Australia and found the seek.com.au website. This was long before the time of high-speed internet so I used a dial-up modem and took over the family landline for the evening. I applied for thirty-odd roles in southeast Queensland, received eighteen-odd responses and set up interviews with thirteen recruitment agencies/companies for late November/early December 2005 during which I would take a 'Look, See, Feel' tour. I was going to make this happen. We were getting out of East London and out of South Africa.

One of the roles I applied for was on the Gold Coast (GC), 60 kilometres south of Brisbane. The recruiter (Mike) emailed back stating that he was from East London and had attended Selborne. He advised that his dad had even been deputy mayor of East London for a period. If that wasn't fortunate enough, he had married Karen's cousin, Sue, which we would find out later. After some family negotiating, Mike and Sue put me up for the two-week visit. What I didn't realise was that Mike hardly slept – falling asleep most nights on his recliner for only a few hours – and that he liked beer. This meant late nights with Mike – occasionally interrupted by Sue sleepwalking, followed by Mike enthusiastically telling her to go back to bed – and then long days on the train up to Brisbane for interviews. Walking around Brisbane CBD in a suit with a backpack on, I felt like Balki Bartokomous from *Perfect Strangers*[23], spending more time looking up at the buildings than on the street level. To borrow another phrase, it was like: 'You're not in Kansas/East London anymore, Grantie.' I would end up landing a role at PwC in Brisbane through the network of firms, start date to be confirmed but certainly in the first quarter of 2006. Mission accomplished.

In between completing the Ironman and heading to Australia in November, I would be made redundant for the first time. I had been working for Da Gama Textiles as the financial accountant for the Small Business Division (SBD). The SBD consisted of nineteen retail stores across three companies and two countries (SA and Namibia). In January 2005, a fifty-year trade embargo was lifted on Chinese exports. No one could have predicted how

---

[23] *Perfect Strangers* was a sitcom that aired in South Africa from the mid-1980s to early 1990s. Balki was the Eastern European cousin to an American, trying to navigate American culture.

quickly they would re-enter the South African textile market. Landing on our shores at below our cost price, it decimated the SA textile industry and a quarter of our thousand-plus workforce was made redundant in the first five months of the year. In the weeks following the redundancy, a recruitment agent I met with advised: 'You're white, you're male, you'll struggle to get a job,' further re-enforcing our decision to leave South Africa.

I would spend the redundancy payment on an engagement ring.

Karen and I got engaged in August 2005 and the wedding date was set for 14 January 2006. I was doing contract work again at PwC while completing various accounting credits required to commence the chartered accountancy program in Australia. I was driven.

In the meantime, there was the wedding to plan for. I would learn a valuable lesson of the difference between table settings and table seatings! A final total of over 150 guests attended the ceremony and reception at Two Swans on a wonderful day of celebrations. Most guests gave a financial contribution toward the big move to Australia, all of which went to the cost of shipping the container of our meagre worldly belongings to Queensland.

Unfortunately, the honeymoon was postponed as I had to prep for two supplementary exams just over a week after the wedding. In what was an emotional week, I wrote an exam on Monday 23 and again on Wednesday 25 January 2006, packed our container with all our belongings on Friday 27 and received the news that I had passed both exams that afternoon. What a week! With our furniture on its way to Australia, the newly married couple moved in with my parents as we waited for the migration paperwork to be processed.

These were not easy days, but they certainly were exciting!

CHAPTER EIGHT

TRAUMA THREE – LEAVING MY HOMELAND

March 2006 was always going to be a big month. Leaving Mum was always going to be tough. I was the eldest. I was the driver in the car. I was leaving.

With flights booked on the 'migration package' with Singapore Airlines (which allows extra baggage), we were to depart East London for Brisbane in the middle of the month. Various family and friends came to the EL airport to wish us on our way. Hugging my mum goodbye was traumatic for both of us. Through her tears, she said: 'I just want you to be happy.' It was such a beautiful thing to say.

Luckily, we had friends on the domestic flight to Johannesburg who took some of our luggage, as South African Airways did not provide us with the extra baggage allowance for the domestic leg of the trip. This would not be the last of our baggage 'luck'. Checking in at international departures at OR Tambo Airport, we were greeted by a tall, skinny, gold-toothed indigenous African man. He informed us that the 'migration package' baggage allowance was only for one leg of the trip (i.e. just to Singapore) and did not apply to the final leg on to Brisbane. That cost, he advised, would be just over R4,000 (AUD650).

It had already been an emotional day for Karen and I, saying goodbye to our parents just hours earlier. Now, in the middle of the queue at international departures, Karen started losing it. We did not even have R4000 capacity on our credit cards. We were in a bind. I explained this in as calm a manner as I was able.

'Wait, wait,' said the gentleman. 'Where are you from?'

'East London,' I responded.

'East London? Oh, you are African. We are all African. We can sort this out.'

There was a lingering silence as I processed what he had just said, or may have been implying.

'What do you mean we can sort this out? Like a bribe?' I said, thinking there were cameras watching me now, this was a *Carte Blanche*[24] sting. I was done for sure.

'Africa's corrupt. Our president's corrupt. Mbeki's corrupt. It's okay,' said Mr Gold Tooth.

I just wanted to leave this country and now I was literally about to bribe my way out. Unreal. I pulled out my wallet (which had a few hundred rand in it) and he said, 'Not here. I'll come and find you.'

And with that, he put the tags on our bike boxes and other luggage and sent them down the luggage chute. I watched as they disappeared out of sight and wondered when, if ever, I would see them again. Karen and I looked at each other and went through security to passport control.

What were we going to do? Was this a set-up? What if we didn't give him enough money? What if he damaged or put something illegal in our bags?

Who else had he done this with? Was this part of his normal daily working life? What if the plane was hugely overweight and crashed as a result?

---

[24] *Carte Blanche* is like the *60 Minutes/A Current Affair* of South Africa.

After phone calls to the new father-in-law and Mum's boyfriend Nic, I came up with the best plan... Hide! Mr Gold Tooth wouldn't find us in international departures – that place was huge! I was convinced I could hide until it was time to depart and then duck quickly to the gate. I spent almost all of the cash I had buying a Stormers jersey, duty-free alcohol and a few cartons of cigarettes for Mike. I also managed to find a Daily Dispatch newspaper (the local East London paper) to read prior to boarding. I thought it would be good to have an edition from the day we migrated as a keepsake. We found a huge pole to sit behind while biding our time prior to departure. There was no way Gold Tooth would find us here! Ha!

Karen advised she needed to use the bathroom. On the other side of the busy walkway were the toilets. Through the mass of people walking up and down the terminal, I watched the door closing behind her as she entered the women's toilets when he locked eyes on me... Gold Tooth. Fuck.

I was stuck. He found me and I was alone. No witnesses as to what actually occurred at check-in, cameras everywhere. I was probably going to get busted by some authority. He sauntered on over and sat down next to me. I took out the remaining South African rands from my wallet (R140 – about AUD23), fumbled them into the Daily Dispatch and passed them to him. He opened the paper, saw the money, looked at me (almost frustratingly) then at my duty-free purchases, folded up the paper and said, 'There has been a gate change. Please follow me to your new departure gate.'

With that, Gold Tooth stood up, flicked me on the shoulder with *my* Daily Dispatch and faded into the crowd of travellers as Karen returned from the toilet.

'How could you have taken so long?' I asked her rhetorically.

We followed Gold Tooth from a distance, and he literally took my boarding pass as I left African shores.

A very nervous flight to Singapore and then a connecting flight to Brisbane ensued, and we landed a few days before St Patrick's Day. Our luggage arrived at the same time as us and was not tampered with. Anxiety reduced and R140 (AUD23) spent versus R4,000 (AUD650) is a far better story. I just didn't think that I would literally bribe my way out of Africa.

The Commonwealth Games were being held in Melbourne and we had a few weeks to decide where to live in southeast Queensland, prior to starting my Australian business career on 27 March. PwC put us up in a serviced apartment as part of the move.

Migration is hard. You spend so much time and effort to get to the new country, and then the real work starts. Then you actually have to live. You don't know the best mobile phone provider. You don't know clothing stores or where to buy white goods. You don't know that Bunnings is just Servistar[25] on steroids. You don't know energy providers, suburbs or that when people want to meet you for coffee it is just coffee, not something more suggestive that happens sometimes in the movies…

And as for coffee, back then I only knew Nescafe Blend 43. Now in this new world, there were shots and lattes, flat whites and cappuccinos, short and long blacks, almond and skim milk – this was complicated stuff.

We viewed Brisbane as too big a city for us, so we managed to arrange a townhouse on the GC close to Mike and Sue. The GC was where it was at! Now this was living!

The plan was simple: start and complete the chartered accountancy course through PwC, then get a job at Billabong at Burleigh Heads on the GC. Mic drop! Why not a white picket fence and two little sons to complete the picture? Oh well,

---

[25] Servistar was the largest hardware store in East London.

best-laid plans and all that.

The daily train trip up to Brisbane would be an inconvenience for sure; however, it would only be temporary – as is all of life. At just over an hour each way, if you got a seat, it was not too bad, I told myself.

The first days at the new job were a whirlwind. I met Brian, one of the Partners in the Advisory practice, on day two. He did not like the South Africans he had met previously and may even have expressly asked if I was of English or Afrikaans descent. He said that the Brisbane Advisory team had a surf club and every Wednesday they went down to Main Beach on the GC and surfed. He asked if I was keen... of course I was! Signing us up on the spot, we were to be picked up at 4.45 the following morning.

I excitedly told Karen that night, who was not impressed. 'Grant, you aren't that good! They are probably all pros,' she said. 'This is going to be so embarrassing.' And so it went.

Arriving at the Spit[26] that Wednesday morning was surreal. I was living in Australia, at work, surfing with my new teammates in the middle of the week. The surf school only had foam-top nine-foot boards. It was onshore, with hardly any swell. And although I had previously thought that standing up was my trick, in comparison to the rest of the group, I was Kelly Slater. When we returned to the office later that day, I had suddenly become the surfer in the office – high praise indeed!

While I was gainfully employed, Karen struggled to get a job, eventually waitressing down at Marina Mirage[27]. It is tough being qualified and not even being interviewed for roles. This is a lesson I would also learn on a number of occasions in Australia. Fortunately, despite only starting at PwC in late March, I was promoted to the

---

[26] The Spit is the breakwater separating Southport from Stradbroke Island on the Gold Coast – about 80 kilometres south of Brisbane.

[27] Marina Mirage is a high-end shopping and dining precinct.

role of senior consultant effective 1 July that year. This was totally out of the blue. I was just so happy to be in Australia and now I was getting a significant pay rise too? Talk about a 'purple patch'. I was a lucky man in the lucky country. We were living the dream!

Karen's immediate response to my unexpected promotion was: 'Congratulations. I'm quitting.'

The waitressing job had been a nightmare and with the increased income from my promotion, she could afford to quit that role and continue to search for a teaching role. With my extra income, Karen was also able to visit her brother in the UK in July, surprising her parents who were travelling from South Africa.

Nic, my mum's long-time boyfriend, would phone over the same period, asking for my mum's hand in marriage. I would cry tears of joy after the call.

In a whirlwind year in which we got married, migrated and started new lives in Australia, I also completed a six-month conversion course in Australian Company Law and Australian Tax to commence the chartered accountancy journey in 2007. To top it all off, our second (onshore) permanent residency application was in the process of being finalised. I was now the primary applicant, as accountants were now on the updated skills shortage list, with teachers dropping off. As a result, I was now required to pass the IELTS exam, the final step for permanent residency. I called the case officer directly and advised that I was already on a 457 visa in the consulting division of a big four accounting firm and could not have been placed in the role had I not been able to speak English.

This being Australia, I was told that those were the rules. The bureaucracy was eye-watering. Apart from the $240-odd expense, there was the wait time required to sit the exam, which was months away for the General Training exam. The Academic exam (which teachers were required to sit and was correspondingly more difficult) had a significantly shorter wait time. I elected to take the Academic exam and passed.

In December, we returned to South Africa for my brother-in-law's wedding. Heading back to my homeland was confronting, confusing and at times traumatic. I had changed.

As Heraclitus stated, 'No man steps in the same river twice, for it's not the same river and he's not the same man.'

Since departing, I had 'Australianised' South Africa and East London in my mind. I had forgotten the unkept sidewalks, the potholes, the taxis hooting and the speeds that people drove. The need to be aware of your surroundings at all times, never to leave anything visible in a car. The people begging at traffic lights or trying to sell you things like black bags and coat hangers at intersections. The car guards and security measures at the banks. The security measures everywhere. The huge economic disparity. The natural sense of order that is almost palpable in Australia was/remains lacking in South Africa. It was an assault on my brain.

The family and friends that remained only added to the complex range of emotions. The familiarity and connections built over decades are not easily forgotten or broken.

After a great Christmas and New Year break, we returned to Australia in late January 2007 where Karen landed a role at a school an hour's drive away from our home in the GC hinterland. We would buy our first home the following month. A 'tropical Balinese oasis' was how it was advertised. We invested at just about the top of the housing boom and the house had only been on the market for a day. We also could only afford it thanks to Karen's new role.

Mum and Nic's wedding date could not be arranged over the December period and was eventually set for 7 April, one week before the anniversary of Dad's accident. I'm not sure Nic was aware, but the Parkins certainly were. I was going to walk my mum down the aisle, a task few sons think they will ever have to do. Although the folks said they would pay for Karen's flight to SA, she declined, citing work commitments in her new role.

April came all too quickly and after the long flight, it was off to my uncle's farm in Mpumalanga. It is a hard part of the country. Coal mining territory. The farm is just outside Breyton, which could be described as a one-horse town where the horse died a long time ago. One road in, one road out, one set of traffic lights. It is most famous as being the birthplace of one of South Africa's greatest Springbok rugby players – Naas Botha. Interestingly, as legend would have it, many years ago the Breyton Sports Club reached out to Naas for some signed memorabilia or the like. His response was, 'Luister vir my, Breyton beteken fokol in my lewe.' Which, translated into English, is, 'Listen to me, Breyton means fuck-all in my life.' Before hanging up the phone.

Driving to the ceremony with my soon-to-be brother-in-law, a Matchbox Twenty song came on the radio. 'It's three a.m. I must be lonely. When she says baby, well I can't help but be scared of it all sometimes. And the rain's gonna wash away, I believe it.'

I was transported to the days preceding and post the accident. The universe is saying it's okay. Dad knows… could he even be watching from somewhere?

Mum and Nic's wedding day would be one of love and warmth, of remembering and creating new memories. On we drove. The ceremony and reception were wonderful, with much love and happiness in the air. Back at the farm, I was given a gentle reminder by Mum's friend Vicki to be present. I had already been getting down about having to head back to Australia the following day.

After emotional goodbyes, I returned to Australia and started the CA program, failing the Tax exam as well as the supplementary exam in the coming months. Such a strong word: 'fail'. I would get very nervous and anxious writing exams. Probably because of not wanting to sit down and let the images of the accident flood my mind. Once sitting and applying myself though, the work was not too much of a problem. Later that year, I managed to pass the Management Accounting exam first time round, which gave me some hope that I was on the right track.

With the end of 2007 approaching, we entered Ironman Western Australia (IMWA), held in the beautiful seaside town of Busselton. The race was just over a week before my next CA exam – Finance and Accounting (F&A). No problem, I am invincible – I've got this. There were multiple motivations for entering the race. So many people at work thought that completing an Ironman was a big deal, and Karen had stated that she wanted to do another Ironman before having children. On some level, I really wanted to start having kids, in part (for sure) because of the accident. So superhuman Grant would be doing Ironman number two and then writing the F&A exam (easily the hardest module of the CA program) just over a week later.

IMWA could only be viewed as a success. Great swim around the iconic Busselton jetty, a sub-six-hour bike ride for 180 kilometres, on a road bike no less (I couldn't afford a triathlon bike). I then waited for an hour in the transition zone to run the marathon with Karen. We finished an hour and a half earlier than our first IM in South Africa two years earlier.

Impossible is nothing after completing an Ironman. Except... the CA F&A exam. The anxiety of waiting for the exam result soured the December break. The post-IM depression was also nothing short of horrendous.

The important things were to pass CA exams, not complete

Ironman triathlons. I failed the exam and the supplementary too. This put a big delay in the plan to work and live on the Gold Coast. Working for Billabong down at Burleigh Heads seemed just a pipe dream.

The PwC Brisbane Surfing Club - circa 2006

CHAPTER NINE

BIG RED MIGRATION

There should have been much to look forward to in 2008. I bought two dogs (Jack Russell cross fox terriers) for Karen's birthday, which were named Jacob and Zuma, after the 'colourful' president of South Africa. Richard and his fiancé had decided to migrate too. In what would become a long-standing joke between us, Richard (my little brother at all of 6'4" and 110 kilograms plus) would recall the days prior to me leaving in early 2006, putting his arm around my shoulder (I'm not quite six feet and a little lighter) and saying words to the effect of: 'Grant, you must go to Australia. It will be good for you. Me, I believe in Africa.' (In my mind, I have him pumping his chest with a clenched fist for dramatic effect.)

My response at the time was a request to just come and see Australia, which they did in December 2007. Six months later, they were starting their new lives in Brisbane.

One weekend in April, I received a knock on the door. It was the neighbour from across the street. He introduced himself and asked if I wanted to buy prawns. Prawns?

What?

Not wanting to piss off a neighbour (even though I don't particularly like prawns), I said 'sure' and wandered across the road with him. I was still waking up from my afternoon nap and he was sorting out the prawns on a scale in the garage. This was probably the first flag I missed.

He had a toddler running around and a huge motorbike and a barrel of something (flags two and three) in his largely unkempt garage. He was nattering on about his fishing escapades and offered me some home-brew white spirits. I said yes and took a sip. He looks at me like he is going to knock my block off.

'You don't sip this, you scull it,' he said as he downed his drink.

I finished the rest in one shot. It was like plane fuel. Head spinning, he asked me if I've ever done pingers.

Pingers? I had no idea what this guy was talking about.

He said, 'Ecstasy.'

I responded that I hadn't and he stated that if I need anything like that, he had underground containers scattered around the Gold Coast filled with the stuff, plus more. He could get me whatever I need. I politely thanked him for the offer (of any illicit drug I may ever need) and the prawns and wandered back across the road. Placing my prawns in the garage fridge, I noticed two South African beers in the door (Carling Black Label, from memory). Head still buzzing from the home-brew shot, I decided this was as good a time as ever to square the ledger – ever the accountant. I took the beers out of the fridge and headed back across the road to the neighbour's house.

He gladly accepted the beer and we continued our chat. While I was standing in his garage, he was looking through his shelves for something, appearing agitated. He found a plastic cup and passed it to me, asking, 'How much do you think that's worth?'

I peered into the cup at what looked to me like rock salt. Ever naïve, I responded that I had no idea.

'That's worth about a grand,' he said as I quickly put the cup (of whatever) onto the barrel (of whatever). Flag number four.

Next moment, my neighbour had a glass pipe that he was burning clean in front me. I had never even seen a glass pipe before, let alone watched someone clean it. He poured two or three pieces of the 'rock salt' onto his hand and then into the pipe and lit up. His eyes rolled up into the back of his head and this dark grey/black smoke came billowing out of his mouth.

The garage door was open to the street and he was smoking (what I later learn is) the drug 'ice' in front of a neighbour he had just met. Meanwhile, his wife was in the house with his toddler wandering around. What was going on?

This… is the Gold Coast Hinterland.

He took another drag on the pipe and more blacky, grey smoke came out his mouth. I was holding my breath as best I could.

'Now I'm not going to sleep for two days,' he said.

I thought, *I really like my sleep. Why would anyone want to do that?*

He offered me the pipe and I declined. Fortunately, he didn't force the issue.

Moments later, Karen came out of our house to run an errand. As I waved her goodbye, I took comfort in thinking that at least the police would know my last whereabouts when they investigate what happened to me.

I managed to get home and after having discussed the incident with Mike, decided to report it to the police. However, a few days later I arrived home to a police car parked on my side of the road, opposite my friendly ice-taking/drug-distributing neighbour. A single officer came out of his house later and I wisely decided not to report it.

July 2008 would be the month of my thirtieth birthday, a natural time to reflect on what I had achieved in the last decade. Despite all the success in completing degrees, migrating, work promotions, home ownership and surviving the trauma of losing Dad, all I could see was failure. I was failing CA exams, was in a part of PwC where I was not successful (I was a truly woeful internal auditor and had missed promotion) and was not living the life I wanted to live. I was also on that train for over two hours a day for the return trip from Helensvale Station to Brisbane. And seriously, it was bullish to call where we were living the Gold Coast! It was still another half an hour to the closest beach from where we lived in Maudsland, which was behind Pacific Pines, which was on the hinterland side of the M1 Motorway, which was behind Helensvale. It felt like the lyric from the Hilltop Hoods song, *1955*: 'I don't tell 'em where I'm from, I tell 'em where I'm close to.' I felt anxious, like I had not achieved enough, like I was failing at life. I also had this nagging question, which could never be answered: What would Dad think?

My thirtieth birthday celebrations were held on Saturday 12 July, made all the merrier by my parents having made the trip over from SA and the Springboks getting a very rare away win against the All Blacks in New Zealand. I have never loved Ricky Januarie's hip so much! Lachlan, an Aussie friend who attended the celebration, said he had never seen anything like it in his life.

Regardless, I felt like I was failing. The CA results and the lack of a promotion during the ordinary annual promotion cycle only re-confirmed it. I was failing at life.

The missed promotion in my mind meant that I was not required or was at least going to be treading water at PwC. I did not tread water; I had a bias for action. I wanted out. Mike lined up an interview for a role with a large franchising company on the Gold Coast. I made it through to the second round of interviews when out of the blue, a Partner in Advisory asked if I was interested in moving into Private Client Services as a manager. This was an out-of-cycle promotion – highly unusual in the firm. The salary package was about the same as the role with the franchising company. Karen literally begged me to take the role on the Coast. I had a choice to make and felt responsible for my career and the direction it should be taking. My big concern was that I had not yet completed the CA program and that once you leave the accounting environment, any new employer would not give you the leeway needed to prepare for the exams. I declined moving forward with the GC role. Interestingly, it was taken up by a fellow PwC employee who did not last three months there, electing to resign without another role to go to. While I felt my decision not to proceed was vindicated, it was definitely a black mark on the ledger with my wife. I would remain at PwC and spend another five years at the firm, gaining valuable work (and life) experience working overseas and at the head office in Sydney.

With my thirtieth birthday celebrations complete, in late July and into August Karen received bad news from SA over consecutive weeks. It got so bad that I did not want her to talk to her mum, dreading those Sunday evening calls. The separate news updates over a four-week period included:
- Her gran having breast cancer
- Two friends having brain cancer
- Her godfather/uncle having an affair

Karen's response to her uncle's affair was to howl like a dog. It was primal. I thought the neighbours were going to come 'round and check if there was domestic violence occurring in the house. I could not believe that she would respond to that news that way. I mean, affairs happen all the time, don't they? And this wasn't an illness, like the other updates.

With the out-of-cycle promotion in late 2008, it felt like my career was (sort of) back on track... and with that came the Global Financial Crisis (GFC). Richard had arrived in Australia with months to spare. Redundancies and reduced work hours hit everyone. However, I had the promotion and a new team to establish. The issue was that Private Clients Services advisory work was a challenge in Queensland ordinarily. Now with the GFC, it was well-nigh impossible. I was sitting in weekly manager meetings reviewing staff utilisation and was consistently the lowest-utilised staff member in the whole division. The staff I was managing were allocated work from other parts of Private Clients Services, but I was standing out like the proverbial sore thumb. I knew I was on the radar (there is always a radar, isn't there?). I was failing again. Bad things can happen really fast, like the dog attack, like the car accident, like another redundancy.

I felt we needed an alternate revenue stream and setting up a migration company seemed the logical step. Friends and colleagues back in SA would no doubt want out of the country, and we could help them. We could certainly provide a better experience than that of the company we had engaged. I had information from that migration company that they were signing up thirty to forty families per month at approximately AUD3,000 each. I wanted a piece of that pie! Their service experience was woeful and I knew we could do a better job. We were also based in Australia as opposed to SA. We could help people on this side when they arrived. This was a far more appealing service offering, at least to me. The plan was for Karen to study and complete the requirements to become a registered migration agent while I registered the company, obtained the necessary insurances and did the marketing and finances. The issue now, going into 2009, was that Australia was not hiring staff from overseas like they were pre-GFC.

Law dictated that we had one year to register as a migration agency after completing the required studies. Although exciting, it was with some degree of fear that we launched Big Red

Migration Agency, named after a type of kangaroo. Establishing Big Red cost about AUD20,000 once the qualification was done, the business registered with ASIC[28] and MARA[29], various insurances paid and the website set up. Never mind, we were in business and now we just needed clients! This key factor to the success of Big Red had been hampered by the GFC. This was my transition out of professional services and Karen's transition out of teaching. We were going to conquer the world... Burleigh Heads and proper living and working on the Gold Coast, here we come!

On the work front, Karen had been fortunate enough to land a role at a prestigious school on the Gold Coast at the beginning of 2009. One of the teachers who had taught her in East London worked there too, and she made friends with a whole new group, including Megan, who taught the same grade as her, and Callum, who also did triathlons, albeit a little bit more competitively than us! This allowed her to put more time into triathlon, even joining a triathlon club.

Things were moving in the right direction, at least on the GC.

In Brisbane, there was my lack of client utilisation at work and the continual failing of CA exams hanging over my head. I had completed three of the chartered accountancy modules and kept failing the Finance and Accounting paper. Out of the blue, a friend in Human Resources (HR) contacted me for a position in Internal Firm Services which suited my skill set. It was a director-grade role and I was merely a newly promoted manager, so I was flattered. After being interviewed by the CFO, no less, I was appointed the role of transition lead or some such title for a significant internal project.

In the coming months, it became apparent that the role was

---

[28] ASIC – Australia Securities and Investments Commission

[29] MARA – Migration Agents Registration Authority

not to formalise the relationship between HR and Finance but with PwC and a third-party vendor. While not what I signed up for, I continued in the position. What alternative did I have?

In what would become a career highlight, I would design and test a system that would run most HR transactions for the Australian firm. I was very fortunate to have a great programmer in Paula who helped develop the system. In essence, it moved various paper-based workflows into electronic workflows, with the added bonus of an audit trail. Now, anyone with access to the system could see the status of the transaction, whether it had been submitted, approved, processed, by whom and on what date. There was now transparency in various end-to-end HR processes where previously there was nothing.

I really didn't think much of it; however, I was quite chuffed that Paula and I had managed to implement it and train various staff on how to use it. Unfortunately, part of the new role also required making the twelve-person Brisbane-based team redundant as an outcome of the vendor engagement. That sucked. I believe about thirty roles also went from the Sydney office.

On completion of the internal project, I returned to Private Client Services on a full-time basis and continued to struggle to make inroads in middle market advisory in Queensland.

At home, we were in a big exercise push. In addition to joining a triathlon club, Karen started using a triathlon coach too and would wait with intent each Sunday night for the gospel to arrive from upon high. While I hadn't yet joined a triathlon club, we did the local gym's twelve-week challenge and intended on doing some triathlons in New Zealand over the Christmas holidays in December 2009. Karen's parents had recently migrated there. We returned from New Zealand in the New Year and after a few days back home on the Gold Coast, I was off to South Africa to launch Big Red Migration and compete in the East London 70.3

Ironman Triathlon. Karen would stay at home due to her school commitments but would be available for phone consultations if required. It was a very busy and exciting time.

I could not begin to imagine what 2010 had in store...

Launching Big Red was the start of a long-term goal of financial independence. That independence relied on customers – one-off customers at that. Once migrated, Big Red's services were redundant. When I arrived in East London that January, I put adverts in the Daily Dispatch and on Facebook and interviewed many, many people in person. Two things became apparent very quickly:

1. People were desperate to get out of South Africa
2. Most of them would not meet the strict requirements for migrating to Australia

I could tell within minutes of meeting potential Big Red customers whether they could get into Australia or not. And by far, the majority could not. I recalled a friend's advice in preparing the initial financial forecast. He declared that the most consistent error entrepreneurs make is to significantly overestimate revenue and understate expenses. With that in mind, I had reduced my initial target to four clients for what was anticipated to be the first of many trips back to SA. Big Red ended up with one client from that trip, sourced via the in-laws – an Old Andrean and his girlfriend no less.

On the triathlon side, having just competed in a few races in NZ and the twelve-week gym challenge, I was in pretty good racing shape for the East London 70.3 Ironman being held while I was there. I went down to Orient Beach in the days preceding the race to register and was taken aback by the race number assigned to me. The number was 567.

This was part of the number plate of the Mercedes Benz that I was driving in 1998 (full registration number BBD 567 EC) and

Dad passed away in. My initial thoughts were to ask for another race number. Then I thought that it was a sign from the universe that Dad would be watching this one. He was around…

I had entered many, many events since the accident, and many since that 70.3 race, and I have never received that race number again. Phil was going to be watching as he always did. In hot, humid and windy conditions, I got a personal best time for the 1.9 kilometre swim, 90 kilometre bike and 21.1 kilometre run, completing the course in well under six hours.

A little deflated from the lack of converted customers, I returned to Queensland to find my wife fully immersed in the triathlon club scene. There is nothing like a good cult. She would leave very early for morning sessions and arrive back late at night to eat and sleep.

As I still had the final two CA courses outstanding (including my nemesis – Finance and Accounting) and had been the primary driver in establishing Big Red, there was no chance I could put in the training volume required to compete in events on the Gold Coast through the rest of summer. I had enough on my plate with work, CA studies and trying to source customers for Big Red. I had done my sub-six-hour 70.3 triathlon and now it was time to focus on other (and in my mind, more important) things.

Karen, though, was laser-focused. Measuring food, entering races up and down the coast and training, training, training. Eat, sleep, train. Repeat. I supported her in the purchase of a AUD5,000 road bicycle to help improve her triathlon performances. While the effort and application were admirable, I did not think it was sustainable and wanted to know when it would end. In the almost ten years of doing events together, we would go through these peaks and troughs of training, so I assumed this was just another training peak. Karen bluntly advised that the new training regime was not going to change.

She was now a triathlete.

In April I finally received a passing result for the Finance and Accounting module that I had failed four times previously. I celebrated a bit hard that Friday night and the following night at my good friend Clayton's thirtieth birthday. Karen had (another) triathlon on the Sunday morning and although I needed to purge some excess fuel on the way there to watch the race, I still went to watch her compete.

Clayton would later describe my relationship with my wife as like ships passing in the night. I would sarcastically state that my wife now belonged to the Littil Church (being an acronym for Life Is Triathlon, Triathlon Is Life). Regardless, I now had one exam left until I became a Chartered Accountant and the rest of our lives could begin. I would write that exam in June.

I also continued trying to get additional clients in for Big Red Migration, although this was becoming increasingly difficult with the amount of time Karen (who was the registered agent) was spending away from home.

June also welcomed the arrival of more overseas visitors. This time to live with us. Karen's brother, his wife and two kids under the age of two had migrated to Australia after spending a few years in the UK and South America. This made for an interesting dynamic as I felt I lost my home. They ended up staying for four months and as my wife was never at home, I was the host. Jacob and Zuma were petrified of the children, and even the main bedroom and ensuite bathroom were not off limits to the young children's exploits. I would fish a coffee mug, a dog's bone and my alarm clock out of my ensuite toilet over a three-week period, strategically placed there by one (or both) of the infants.

Still, Karen trained.

She called me in late June with much excitement – another teacher was unable to make the school trip to the Victorian snow fields and she could attend for free. All she would need was some warm clothing. I stated that she absolutely had to go and $300 worth of winter clothing later, Karen was off. She advised that it may be difficult to contact her over the period due to the variety of events that had been arranged for the students and potential lack of mobile phone reception. I was just genuinely happy that she was happy and excited, and giving herself a break from all the triathlon training.

It was indeed difficult to contact her over the period and it was a challenge being the host to my in-laws. It was a big change to go from two adults and two dogs in the house to adding another two adults and two small kids. Put simply, I was outnumbered.

At the end of the week, I drove the forty-five minutes down to the Coolangatta Airport to pick Karen up. In the terminal, my 'spider senses' suddenly went off. Through the busyness and noise and action of the arrivals lounge, I felt like something wasn't right. It really felt like I was on the outside of a joke. A joke that was on me. I saw several male teachers, looked at one in particular and caught myself thinking, *Is there something going on here?*

It was a horrible thought – surely not. I quickly pushed it out of my mind. Despite being away for the week and having virtually no contact with her husband, Karen also appeared disengaged and distant. I put it down to her being tired from the big week of snowy activities. However we would have an argument in the airport parking lot about my buying Bon Jovi tickets for us that she viewed as too expensive. She had not been contactable when I booked them and had seen Bon Jovi in 1995. I was only trying to do a good thing for us. We took the long drive back to the house in virtual silence. A house that didn't feel like our home anymore.

On Friday 9 July 2010 I got the news that I had passed the last outstanding CA exam. Finally, I was a Chartered Accountant!

The course I had started in 2007 was finally done. A journey that had formally commenced in 2004 was now complete. I was a Chartered Accountant – just like my dad was.

I will never forget my wife's comment from across the kitchen bench when I shared my exciting news with her.

'Congratulations,' she said disingenuously. 'You must be so proud.'

This was the culmination of years and years worth of work and that was the response I received from my life partner. My brother-in-law was genuinely more animated and happier for me.

My thirty-second birthday was on the Sunday and even though we had the house to ourselves for a period and Karen had made an effort to get some gifts, there were no birthday 'celebrations'. In fact, there had been none of that since before the Victorian ski-trip in June. Physically, it was like she had gone cold, like my touch repulsed her. I would ask her in bed one night if she was having an affair. A horrible question to ask your wife. She would deny it.

The day after my birthday, Karen said she wanted to start counselling. I typed this diary note the following day on 13 July:

'Pretty tough come down yesterday… finally pass CA, have thirty-second birthday and get told by missus that she wants to go into marriage counselling and is thinking about divorce.

I am the reason she has been training so hard (and therefore the reason she is hardly at home) and she does not think she wants kids. Hmm, nice one. She does not like how her next five years are currently looking. (I have little doubt that having John, Kate and two small kids is not helping.)

From my side, I am not sure I even know her anymore. She trains, teaches and sleeps. Every Sunday evening, she sits and waits for her weekly program from her triathlon coach (let's call him Pastor Craig – he might as well be) and is up at 4 a.m., out of the house by

4.30ish every day – including weekends. Because I have to catch the train, I cannot attend any weekday sessions with her. She is generally in bed by 7.30 p.m. and I arrive at 6.45 p.m. on a normal night. That is apart from the nights that she trains (usually Tuesday and Thursday) and then she gets back at about 7.45 p.m. and is in bed by 8.15 p.m.

Weekends now pan out like this. Typical 4 a.m. wake up and cycling by 5 a.m. Finish at 9 a.m. if you are lucky (sometimes by 11 a.m. if you are really unlucky – I was on one ride like this). Go home to sleep and then be in the pool back in Southport by 3.30 p.m. for an afternoon swim. This swim is typically 1–1.5 hours and then it is home to eat and sleep – usually in bed by 7.30 p.m. to 8 p.m. again, bearing in mind this is a Saturday night. There really is no time at all for anything else on a Saturday. Sunday morning is another 4 a.m. start and a run of usually 18–24 kilometres. Followed by a swim and then wait... a barbeque – because no one has families – or wants to go home to them (as I found out last night). This has been going on since January.

Pastor Craig and I don't really see eye to eye (and the rest of the squad might as well be his disciples – it is quite painful) and he was fired from Karen's school for physically abusing a kid (he threw a pool buoy at the kid in some sort of a rage). Karen's triathlon friend from school (and a world champion – Callum – a nice guy) does not see eye to eye with Craig either – but it means nothing.

There is naturally an interesting mix of people in the triathlon, one gentleman (Ronnie) currently lives in a camper van in the trailer park and quit his job because he didn't like it. He kind of just floats around now and Karen has mentioned this as being pretty cool on some level. (Obviously, her 'five-year vision' of herself currently involves a lot more responsibility than this guy.)

I am not sure I have been this far apart from my wife since when we broke up between 1998 and 2000 (as young kids). I could not *sleep last night between 2.15 a.m. and 4 a.m. (just before she got up). We used to walk the dogs together every night – now that may occur once every two weeks or so. I walk them alone most nights.*

It is quite clear that there is a long road ahead if indeed it is taken at all. I am not alone in questioning this triathlon drive. Her family and friends are also questioning it – her old friends at least. Her folks are now coming over for a while but she does not appear to be listening to anyone at the moment, so I am not sure if talking to them will make a difference at all.

To add to this, we started Big Red Migration (which was really all me – all Karen did was study) and I have been committed to getting that off the ground. I am definitely guilty of pushing that too hard on her – but after spending $8000 studying it, we had to have a go.

From my side, I have invested a significant portion of my life with this girl, but I am fully aware that the sun will rise again, so let's see – but at the moment I am not getting my hopes up. It is what it is…'

CHAPTER TEN

TRAUMA FOUR - BETRAYAL

Counselling commenced in late July. We met the counsellor in Southport for an initial visit where we were asked how invested we were to make the marriage work. My wife responded first and stated thirty per cent. I stated the same as I just didn't feel like I knew her at all anymore.

It would be our first and last counselling session together as a couple.

I would continue to walk Jacob and Zuma each night on my own. My wife was never at home, or had enough energy when she was, to walk them down the hill to the park and let them get their exercise. Walking them also got me out of the house, which I felt I had lost to my brother-in-law and his family.

Life was pretty shit. I was working in Brisbane, which required travelling almost three hours a day. I was in marriage counselling with a wife I never saw. I had my in-laws living with me and I was naïvely trying to start a migration business with a business partner who did not appear invested at all. Over the coming weeks, I would do some work for a client in Townsville, North Queensland. I stayed in the casino there and naturally felt the need to check out the facilities. I felt sad and sorry for myself and after getting on a bit of a roll at the blackjack table, winning couple of hundred dollars, I cashed in, well up for the evening. I was walking out of the casino when I asked myself why I was leaving? I was only going to mope alone upstairs in my room. Why not play with the winnings? What does it matter? I turned around and went back in.

I finished the night $1800 up, much happier for taking the chance. I wanted to tell my wife when I got home but decided that I would keep it quiet and look to book an overseas trip for us when things got sorted. Just the two of us. Of course, they would get sorted, wouldn't they? Relationship issues happen all the time... don't they?

To add more complexity to the mix, the parents-in-law came to stay with us from late July until early August. That is what our marriage (which was already in therapy) needed... more people in our space. Richard had a birthday gathering on Saturday 7 August, which I attended on my own as Karen had a school function on the same evening. Late that night, she SMSed me, stating that she had had too much to drink and was going to stay at her friend Megan's house. I was glad that she was having a nice evening and stated as much in my response to her.

She arrived back home mid-afternoon the following day, which I thought was disrespectful to her parents who were returning to New Zealand just a few hours later. I hugged her upon her return. She was cold.

With her parents back in New Zealand, my depressing existence continued. I did have a public holiday to enjoy that week though. Ekka[30] public holiday for Brisbane (but not the Gold Coast) was on Wednesday 11 August. For those outside

---

[30] Ekka Show Day is a regional public holiday on Queensland. It is typically held annually in Brisbane on the second Wednesday of August. The public holiday date differs throughout the state, with the Gold and Sunshine Coasts having their public holiday on a different day, often on a Friday to make it a long weekend.

Australia, it is an unusual public holiday in Queensland where the 'City meets the Country'. Inspired by the counsellor during the previous night's session, I went to see lawyers on the Gold Coast to discuss divorce. This was certainly not how I ever saw myself spending a public holiday; indeed, it was an exercise I never thought I would ever undertake at all. However, I could only go on behaviours – and what were my wife's behaviours indicating, Grantie?

My wife was never at home and had not been herself for months. After seeing the lawyers earlier in the day, I was ready to have a direct conversation with her that evening when she eventually returned home. It didn't matter whether she was tired or had to wake up early the next morning to train. This conversation had to happen now. That night, I sat her down in the lounge and we discussed her behaviour. Her brother and family waited awkwardly in a bedroom down the passage.

I asked a huge question. A question I never thought I would have to ask: 'Do you want to be in this marriage or not?'

'I don't know,' came the response.

'Well, then you need to go,' I said.

Silence filled the vacuum where filler words may have previously. We were in uncharted territory.

Yes, Karen, this is real. She looked at me with a sense of bewilderment, as if the horrific status quo of the current existence could continue forever. I wanted someone who wanted to make the sacred institution of marriage work with me. It was not an 'I don't know' equation to me.

'Where will I go?' she asked.

'I don't know. It's not my problem.' It felt good to finally be standing up for myself.

After speaking to her brother, my wife left with a bag of clothes. Her brother and his family stayed on.

The adrenaline rush of taking a stand quickly dissipated and the loneliness and isolation returned. We were supposed to be flying up to Yeppoon that weekend where Karen was going to do a 70.3 Ironman Triathlon. I was going to go up for support as I had been focused on Big Red, work and finishing the CA course.

Do I still go? What are we doing? I decided not to fly up and Karen agreed. She would drive up with some members of her triathlon cult (oh, sorry, I meant club). I was so beside myself after asking her to leave the house on the Wednesday evening that I did not go to work on the Friday. The range of emotions and complexities of the situation were taking a toll on my emotional and mental wellbeing.

I had been receiving advice from my sister-in-law regarding the relationship issues. She was at home all day with her two young boys, in a new country, and her sister-in-law had literally left the building. On her prompting, I called the counsellor, quite distressed, and was on the phone with him when I heard loud dance music coming from the driveway. It was Karen with two of her triathlon friends – Callum and Matt. They were commencing their trip up to Yeppoon. It sounded more like a party trip than a triathlon one, at least to me. Karen bounded out of the car and changed physically from this excited, bubbly person to one in shock when she saw me opening the front door. It was like the blood drained from her cheeks. She had expected me to be at work.

Karen collected whatever items she needed for the triathlon and I helped them tie down their bikes properly onto our vehicle – the vehicle we had bought as part of establishing Big Red Migration. I wished them on their way, shaking Callum's hand in the process and giving Karen a hug. They were going to be driving halfway up to Yeppoon that day, racing on the Sunday and then driving the full distance back to the Gold Coast on the Monday.

I almost flew up on the Saturday to support her. She was still my wife, after all. It felt terrible being so powerless. I decided against it when I sat with the thought that she had just moved out of the house on the Wednesday night and still decided to do a triathlon hundreds of kilometres away.

What sort of priorities were these? What are the behaviours indicating?

Race day came and went and I decided that if Karen did not return to the family home early upon arrival back on the Gold Coast, I would pack up all the rest of her things. She didn't and so I did. When she did arrive back late that week, all available bags were packed with the remainder of her clothes and waiting for her at the front door. I would spend the next two weeks seeing the counsellor, trying to talk to my wife while continuing to live with my in-laws, who had now been staying in our house for almost three months.

On Tuesday 31 August, I received the electronic phone bill for both of our mobile phones. It was only marginally higher than usual, and I was interested as to whether that was due to my getting the latest iPhone the previous month. It wasn't.

It wasn't my bill that was higher than usual. It was Karen's. That was weird, I thought. I might just have a quick look into that. There, in black and white, were the call and SMS logs. Between the call and SMS logs, there was one number that kept showing up.

It was not mine… I started to feel sick.

I checked the previous month's bill. Same thing… same number, not mine.

I checked the month before that. Same thing… same number, not mine.

There were sixty-plus contacts each month going back to the June holiday. I didn't know what to do. I called Mike, explained to him what I had found and asked if he knew how to track a mobile number in Australia. He said he'll call me back.

Mike called me back less than five minutes later. 'It's Callum's. I just typed the number into Google.'

I was dumbstruck. Callum. The fellow teacher at Karen's school. I had shaken his hand and wished him safe travels to the Yeppoon triathlon just a few weeks ago when he travelled up with Karen in our car. He had visited our house, including for a Christmas in July party which doubled as my birthday party. We had watched him compete in a triathlon on the Broadwater and had celebrated an Australia Day with him. It appeared my wife and Callum have been doing a different kind of celebrating.

The auditor in me came out. I highlighted the calls and the dates and recounted where I was by reconciling it to my work calendar. Sunday nights when I was in the lounge hosting her sibling and his wife, Karen was in the bedroom SMSing Callum.

When I had been in Townsville for work, multiple contacts. And the best… on the night I asked her to leave the family home, when Karen had stated that she was going to stay at Megan's house, Callum's phone number was the only one on the call and SMS log.

I simply could not believe it, but the proof was there in the logs.

With this data, I moved from auditor into full execution mode, calling my estranged wife and stating that I needed to see her urgently at Westfield Helensvale that evening. Incredibly, I got some cooperation from her and she agreed to meet. On the train trip home, I bumped into her brother. I showed John the four months' worth of phone bills and analysis, highlighted and referenced to the whereabouts of both of us over the period. He was silent, shaking his head. What could be said anyway? It was a long train trip down the coast. John went straight to the house while I went to the coffee shop for the showdown/date with destiny – whatever you want to call it – with Karen.

Zarraffa's Coffee was closing for the night by the time I got there. I ordered a takeaway flat white and walked across the road to the Thai restaurant, where waiters were putting out tables and chairs for the evening trade. I chose the table furthest away from the restaurant and sat and waited. People were coming and going with shopping bags of groceries, others were in their gym gear, having attended a session upstairs at the Goodlife gym. I was slightly envious as I imagined how their lives may be, juxtaposed with how messed up mine felt right now. I could hear the clanging of metal chairs behind me as they were separated from each other and laid out on the plaza. Karen arrived and we exchanged the barest of civilities. I had my work file on the table with four months' worth of proof of something. The jig was up.

After abrupt introductions were exchanged, I quickly asked, 'So, Karen, when you left the house on that Wednesday night, where did you go?'

'To Megan's,' she responded.

'Are you sure?'

'Yes.'

Pause.

'Okay, well, that is interesting,' I said.

'Why?'

'Well, how did she know you were coming?' I asked.

Blank face… long stare.

'What do you mean, Grant?'

'Well, you never called her… so how did she know you were coming to stay that night?'

In Afrikaans, they would say, 'Het jou katvis!' which, translated, means, 'Got you, catfish!'

I had now caught the liar in the act. What had happened to our relationship that it would all come to this sort of behaviour?

I answered my own question.

'You called someone that night, didn't you? And it wasn't Megan,' I prompted.

'Yes,' came Karen's reply.

'And who was that?' I asked, knowing full well who and just wanting to hear the words from her mouth.

'Callum.'

A sound from deep in my soul instantaneously exited my mouth as I looked up to the stars and the tears began. I felt breathless, deceived, betrayed and cheated. I was all these things…

I don't recall how the interaction was wound up as she skulked back into the night… back to Callum's lair. I remember calling Richard, Ross, Mike, Dale and Clayton to join me at the closest restaurant (Outback Jack's) as I drank my way into oblivion.

A few hours of solid drinking with my friends ensued. Ross advised that he had been trying to get hold of me as he had heard rumours via his social circles. We all ended up back at my home where my in-laws stayed in their room and we continued drinking and playing guitar. In an alcohol-fuelled and bitter haze, I wanted to put a Facebook status up, declaring to the world the injustice and deceit I had just discovered. I wanted the cheater to share the embarrassment that I felt. I wanted her to hurt like I was hurting.

I was wisely talked out of it and merely changed my status from 'married' to 'single'. Karen's aunt made an online comment that I was joking. Unfortunately, I was not.

I woke up on 1 September 2010 to a new beginning. My new reality…

I had discovered the affair and again, my view of the world was reinforced: bad things happen. Dog attacks, car accidents, betrayal. Horrendously hungover and even more heartsore, I wept. I even phoned Karen's old teacher who also worked at the school that morning, asking if he knew about the affair. He didn't.

I felt like the laughingstock of the Gold Coast and there was no way I could go to work. I would take many days off over this period of mourning. And out of pure spite, I would drive to a surfboard shaper and order a custom-made board. The $1800 that I had put aside for us to holiday and rekindle our relationship would now be spent on me.

And I wept… every day… for twenty-three days straight, I wept. I wept in the shower. I wept at home. I wept on the train up to Brisbane. I wept in the office. On the train back down to the Gold Coast, on the walk into the office. In the gym, at social gatherings, everywhere.

One morning, I wept so much driving to the train station that I could not see out the windscreen, no doubt bringing back the traumatic memories of the car accident with Dad.

I knew I had to keep exercising for my own sanity. I went to the gym early one morning where one of the effervescent instructors enthusiastically asked, 'And where is your beautiful wife this morning?'

I stated she had run off and had an affair as the tears started again in the middle of the gym. Just one of many triggers I would experience in the coming months.

The marriage counselling sessions transitioned to counselling sessions with immediate effect. On reflection, this was where I would do some of the hardest work. The counsellor was a slightly older gentleman, and he would give me homework such as listing the emotions I was feeling. Naming the emotions helped a lot and I think he was quite impressed when I took out my phone the following session and went through the list of emotions I had been experiencing. I did not keep the list; however, I'm sure it would have included many of the following: disappointed, betrayed, heartbroken, taken for granted, sad, jaded, shocked and disillusioned.

My ego was severely bruised. My relationship with Karen had been a fairy tale. Together as teenagers, a few years apart and then re-connecting. For almost a decade, we had been a team. We started a rowing club together... we did Ironman triathlons together... we migrated together... we started a migration company together. We were husband and wife, FFS...

I was unnecessarily harsh on myself for being so blind to the affair. You have to trust someone. Your life partner should be one of these. Added to that, my wife's response two short years earlier to her uncle's shenanigans totally removed any thought of there being an extramarital affair. It was horrible to feel so deceived, so betrayed.

'What will people think?' I asked the counsellor.

'What other people think of you is none of your business,' was the response.

Pause.

'What other people think of you is none of your business,' he repeated. 'She moved on a long time ago, Grant. You are just mopping up. You are playing catch-up.'

I didn't like being behind in a race I didn't even know I was in. Not only was I playing catch-up, but I was also trying to reconcile when it all began – typical behaviour of someone who has experienced betrayal trauma. Some answers you really don't want to know.

After day twenty-three, my tears were an every second or third-day occurrence. In terms of the five stages of grief, my shock and denial had turned into a state of bargaining. Was I really prepared to let the relationship go? Was my wife really sure she wanted to let it go? Did she perhaps think she had made a mistake and was too nervous to acknowledge it? We had been through so much together.

My parents-in-law, also taking strain over the affair, were providing advice too.

'You need to be sure it is over,' was the message I received. My father-in-law even stated that I should call Callum and ask him what was going on, which I did. Callum cut the conversation short and sent me a SMS soon after, which I copied into a journal at the time:

'Grant, by calling you is only allowing myself to cop abuse and will not accomplish anything. Yes, I feel crap about this situation and sorry for the pain you are in being separated from Karen. Problems have been spoken to me quite frequently since knowing you both. I refused to get involved and never wanted to. However, over the past month I have cracked and gone against your trust in me and could not suppress the feelings I had for Karen. This is what I apologise for because the three of us are hurting but you must feel very upset. I have never spoken a bad word (about) you and have left Karen to make her own mind up. Yes, I should have waited till the divorce was official but I couldn't.'

Divorce was official? Wow! Like the counsellor said: she really had moved on a long time ago and I was just playing catch up. It was naïve to think a conversation with Callum would suffice.

Over the next few weeks, I would send roses with chocolates to my wife's school each Friday. I didn't know where she lived anymore so this was the easiest way to show I still cared and was prepared to try to reconcile. To add further complexity, our citizenship ceremony date was set for early October. I stated that regardless of the current situation, we should attend the ceremony together as it was the completion of a journey we had started in 2003. In one of the few positive interactions I had with her, she agreed to attend.

Dad's birthday was on 12 October. It would have been his sixtieth and oh, how I missed him. Oh, how I felt I had failed him, how I longed for his guidance. Karen had taken Jacob and Zuma and the in-laws had since moved out. I was alone in a four-bedroomed house in no man's land in the hinterland of the Gold Coast. I took the day off work and stayed at home. While the daily weeping had subsided, I was particularly down that day. Cristiano, a Chilean colleague of mine phoned to check in. I told him I wasn't in a good place at all. Lots of tears were shed.

The following day, my estranged wife and I became Australian citizens. She was living with her new lover. Ross and Richard attended, with Ross, in particular, being very well-behaved. Having received mixed (at least in my mind) messages in relation to my efforts to reconcile, I had written Karen a letter, which I gave to her after the ceremony. We spoke for a long time afterwards and I got the distinct impression that she was having mixed feelings about the affair. I urged her to think about whether it was what she really wanted and left the conversation with some hope that all was not lost. I also reiterated that I was happy to help subsidise for her to live on her own for a while, to allow her to come to her own decision.

I was drinking a lot, missing work and going to see the counsellor. As the counsellor said, I was playing catch-up. My wife had moved on a long time ago. I simply felt blindsided. My brain kept replaying interactions and behaviours, which now all seemed so clear. I was angry with myself for not seeing it.

Thursday 14 October ended up being my 'Come to Jesus' moment. The number fourteen being synonymous now with my dad's passing (14 April) and my failed marriage (14 January – our wedding day). Having mourned Dad and feeling like I had disappointed his memory (and what a bizarre thing to think in the first place?), I had just finished a lunch break run and was getting changed back into my work kit when Brian called.

'Hey, Grant, how are you?' he asked in his strong Scottish accent.

'I'm pretty fucked Brian,' came my response.

'Look, I'm available for a coffee later this afternoon. It would be great to catch up.'

Brian and I met for coffee where he gave me the 'pull up your socks' talk that I needed.

'You didn't cause this, Grant,' he said. 'You were acting with the best of intentions at all times.'

True.

'She wanted a taste of something else and she went and got it. In all those work trips away, you could have done the same and you didn't. You were always the driving force in the relationship. She would not have gotten to Australia if it wasn't for you. Leaders take responsibility and you have done so in this case, but you are not responsible for her actions. She had an itch and she wanted it scratched.'

Epiphany. Light bulb moment. Call it what you will. Over the coming hours, Brian's advice sank in and once it had, everything changed. Everything changed because <u>my view of the world changed</u>.

I would be responsible for how I handled myself going forward and would no longer take on the unnecessary guilt of a failed marriage. I <u>had</u> been acting with the best of intentions. I was doing the CA and starting Big Red Migration <u>for us</u>. I hadn't strayed. Why should I suffer? This was not my responsibility to own.

CHAPTER ELEVEN
FRASER ISLAND AND A FUTURE UNWRITTEN

I went surfing with Ross and Dale the next morning before work. Dale was getting married the following weekend on Fraser Island. Karen and I had declined the invitation as it was the weekend before the Noosa Triathlon. (Looking back, we were very serious amateur triathletes.) My focus had since changed (just slightly!) since that initial decline. Ross stated I should ask Dale if I could still attend. As I paddled across to ask, Dale pre-empted my request and suddenly, I was going to Fraser Island for a wedding.

With my (Brian-enabled) mindset change, I would have an awesome weekend on the Gold Coast, randomly catching up with an old work colleague and having a night out with him on Australia's Glitter Strip. We ended up being the first males allowed into Shuck Restaurant in Main Beach, which had just held a (women's only) breast cancer awareness party, feeling like the proverbial fish in the barrel as these inebriated ladies came up to chat to us. It was nice to get some female attention after having suffered at home for so long. I was now looking at the positives again.

I had had a great weekend and for the first time in ages, I was very happy. I think it may have been the first time that

I had truly accepted and more importantly, loved, myself. I was worthy. I was at peace with me and everything that had happened. Dog attacks, Dad's passing, this betrayal. I could do whatever I wanted, as the counsellor had stated. I was as free as I had ever been… no studies, no wife, no animals to look after – just Grantie. Enough moping, we didn't have kids together – this was no longer on me. It felt good. And I was going up to Fraser Island with good friends the following weekend for Dale and Cath's wedding.

The bigger question was how to get to Fraser Island. Out of spite, yes, that petty emotion, together with not wanting to use too many annual leave days, I used Qantas Club points to book a flight to Hervey Bay, the closest mainland town to Fraser Island. She who shall not be named did not deserve those Qantas Club points so I would use them. I booked the flight for 21 October to meet Ross, Emma and other Gold Coast wedding guests in Hervey Bay that night. We would catch the ferry across to the island the following morning.

Having shed my old skin, I was ready to go that Thursday afternoon. My luggage consisted of a backpack with toiletries, a few t-shirts, boardshorts and a single jersey. Shoes were slip slops, or thongs as they are called in the land down under. With my backpack on, it was time to go to Brisbane Airport. After checking in to the flight, I was going through the security screen when I saw them – two hot little blondes talking to a security officer.

Hot… little… blondes… forever my Achilles' heel. Having no idea where to board a 'Qantaslink' (what is that?) plane, I felt obligated to head on over to said security officer and ask him. It was time for Parks to get back in the game…

As I walked over, the blondes looked like they were leaving the airport. I heard the security officer directing them towards a specific gate for their – you guessed it – Hervey Bay flight.

Now for any of you who haven't been to Hervey Bay, it is God's Waiting Room. When I boarded the flight (a small, twin propeller-driven plane) I simply knew that those blondes were going to the wedding. It was as clear as day. I felt absolutely no need to introduce myself during the flight, partly because I felt no pressure to, partly because it was nice to just observe their goings on. One of them was particularly animated in her interactions with the flight attendant on duty. They could be mates, I supposed.

In a strange twist of fate, I dropped my wallet exiting the plane and failed to introduce myself to them in the arrivals lounge in Hervey Bay. *No matter,* I thought, *I will see them on the ferry tomorrow – I have friends to see here in Hervey Bay anyway.*

The following morning was hot and humid, probably a standard late spring day for the Bay. The sun was ridiculously high and we made it to the ferry with loads of time to spare. In the new way that I had chosen to roll, I did not know how I would get up to Orchid Beach (where the wedding was being held, on the ocean-facing side of the island) but was assured someone would be able to give me a lift. Sure... whatever... details. I also would be sorting out my own sleeping arrangements. Ross was lending me a tent and there was a campsite two kilometres up the beach from the small Orchid Beach township. I had no pillow and no sleeping bag, which didn't bother me because it should be hot enough anyway. Honestly, none of it mattered to me.

At the ferry, the blondes were nowhere to be seen. And that didn't matter to me either. Oh well, it was a beautiful day. The ferry departed and I was off to see an iconic Australian tourist destination. After a short ferry ride across to the island, I was paired up with Kel (a true Queenslander) in his 4x4 and we commenced the drive up to Orchid Beach. It was chicken soup for the soul for me. I had not driven on a beach since it was banned in South Africa in the early 2000s. Oh, how I had missed it! It was a beautiful day and the tide was low, making for an easy drive.

To top it all off, Kel had many XXXX beers, which he shared with me. We were like kindred spirits as we drank beers while driving on a wide-open beach, heading north up the island. Life was good; my heart was full!

Hours later, we arrived at my campsite. I was suitably hammered from drinking beers most of the day. The wind had picked up and the sun was setting. I was attempting to pitch a tent and managed to arrange a pillow from the mother of the bride, who was also staying in the camp. Having only just managed to set the tent up, it was time to get a lift back to the township for dinner.

Arriving back at the township, I saw people sitting around a fire. Ross and Dale were tending to the BBQ. I scanned the faces across the fire and there they were… I didn't know how they got here, but the blondes were here. Interesting… and… it didn't matter.

I sauntered on over to the boys and a few minutes later, this slight-of-frame blonde came over and introduced herself.

'Hi, I'm Emma,' she said.

I was both flattered and amused. Flattered that this very young-looking woman had introduced herself to me. Amused as Emma was the name of Ross's fiancé, my brother's wife and Dale's ex-wife. You couldn't make this up!

'I'm Grant. We haven't met before. How do you fit in here?'

The wind was swirling around the buildings and Emma appeared physically cold. The age of chivalry was not dead in my book, so I offered up my jersey, which she gladly accepted.

'I've known Cath and Dale for years and have come up to the Gold Coast for too many parties to remember. Christmas,

Australia Day, birthdays. I've even been to Ross and Emma's house many times.'

I wondered how I'd never met her.

'Right, so where are you from then?'

'Melbourne.'

'Ah, makes sense. I saw you in the Brisbane airport last night and thought you and your friend would be coming to the wedding. But I didn't see you on the ferry this morning. How did you guys get to Orchid Beach?'

'Oh, we flew in on a light plane.'

'Wow, that is one way to roll.'

'Yes. The airfield is just behind the dunes over there. We ended up flying across with the wedding cake because someone took up the car seat that was supposed to be reserved for the cake. No pressure at all!'

I decided not to declare that that person was me, chuckling inside.

Oh well!

We shared dinner together and a litre of Absolut Vodka comes out. Ross invented a game called 'Vodka Cocktail Shots' (vodka and cordial is all it is, really) and things got festive.

We move the festivities inside the house due to the mosquitos and midges. It was hot and muggy indoors. I was on an island and enthralled with this enchanting woman. We talked music. She loved Alice in Chains. I told her of my love for Pearl Jam. There was no ego, no 'who is your family?', 'what school did you go to?' bullshit. None of it mattered. I didn't even know what she did for a living. We could have been the only people in the world that evening. I told her about my dad's accident. I didn't tell her my wife had run off with one of her teacher friends. One story was relevant, the other not. One person was literally dead and the other one, figuratively.

I was present and so too was Emma. Totally focused on each other. I told her that I was staying at the campsite up the beach. Emma put her hand on my leg. It was warm.

She advised that all the other women will be staying in another house with the bride and that she will be alone in the house. I am welcome to stay.

Having heard the story of dingos on Fraser Island and even been exposed to the 'dingo got my baby' story in the 1980s, I felt I had a moral obligation to stay the night and protect this damsel in distress. I stayed the night. I would not spend a single night in the tent that weekend. I would not even take the tent down... leaving that task for its owner to do – thanks Ross.

A wonderful wedding ceremony followed the next day, together with some initially awkward interactions between Emma and me. Social/external pressures as we unwittingly became 'those two' at the wedding. Suddenly, and only after allowing the external world in, were there complications. The wonderful social lubricant called alcohol helped reduce that effect that second evening.

With Sunday came departures. I did not have a lift back down the island to the ferry and instead, flew back to Hervey Bay with Emma and another wedding guest, narrowly missing a big tropical storm in the process. Talk about weekend madness!

Emma and I said our goodbyes as I headed to my brother's house in Brisbane. She seemed genuinely keen to see me again, holding onto my jersey as we said awkward goodbyes. I didn't say anything – insurance, I think. She would have to see me again if she kept my jersey!

I spend Monday in the office thinking about the weekend and leave work early to go back down to the GC. I must see Karen to get some paperwork signed for the home loans. She is finally being a bit cooperative. We met in Southport outside a bank branch and once the re-financing papers have been signed, Karen unbelievably asked if I would like to go for coffee.

Wow… coffee.

For months, I had been trying to talk to my wife and now she would like to go for coffee. Just days ago, I met someone who appeared genuinely interested in me. No baggage, no history, just me. Now my estranged wife wanted to talk. Oh, the irony…

I declined the offer. Karen looked at me with a sense of bemusement. I knew I did not need to spend any more time discussing anything with this woman. This shit was done. She walked off and I felt confident. A bit proud, even, of how I handled the situation, of how I'd grown over recent months. We would hardly speak again.

After the bank, I went to visit Mike and Clayton and tell them of the weekend's escapades. They both worked in Southport in the same building. I was wired, talking fast and animated. They were both highly entertained.

The rest of the week was spent recovering from the weekend and it was on to the Noosa Triathlon. The Noosa Tri is certainly the most iconic triathlon in Queensland, if not Australia. I stayed with Brian and his wife Lina and had a few beers the day before the race. I expected the ex to be there, yet was still surprised when I saw her on Hastings Street. It threw me. Another trigger. Lina stated that Brian would react the same way when he would see his ex. I took comfort that this was just something else to work through. Race day came and I raced on anger, with a point to prove. However silly, I wanted to beat her time. She had been doing all this training, weighing food, buying a new bicycle, paying for a coach, etc. I just wanted to smash the course, and of course, have a little fun doing it.

I went just under 2.30 for the 1500 metre swim, 40 kilometre bike and 10 kilometre run race – not bad at all, and just beat her time. Then it was beer and celebrations time. Off to the Noosa

Surf Life Saving Club for a few cleansing ales and a pizza across the road for dinner. I left half a beer on the table and got a taxi to Sunshine Beach at around 10 p.m. It had been a big day.

Brian, Lina and the others had already left to go back to Brisbane so I was alone in the rented accommodation. I had a restless night's sleep. Waking early, I got in the car as the sun was rising and head towards Brisbane on David Low Way. Turning right at Alexandra Headland, I came over a hill and there it was… a Random Breath Test (RBT) station. I felt sick to my stomach and lost the feeling in my legs.

Although the sun was high, it was well before 5.30 a.m. I just felt really tired, didn't I? I couldn't blow over the limit hours and hours after stopping drinking, could I? It was really humid last night and I might have sweated out some of the alcohol.

None of it mattered now as I pulled up to the officer. I had a license for over twelve years and I had never had to do a random breath test. The officer put the breathalyser in my mouth and I blew…

'You're alright, mate, off you go.'

I wanted to ask what the reading was but chose to drive off instead.

I like to think I blew within legal range because I left that half-a-Peroni at the pizza joint. I arrived early in Brisbane and later that day, needed to spend a few hours in the sick bay with a huge headache, probably due to dehydration.

All week, Emma and I called and SMSed each other. She was back in Melbourne and told me she is a flight attendant. We all know what they get up to, don't we? Wasn't that proven on the weekend we met? No, we don't. It was all in my head as I started to make stuff up. Friends were saying that the impending divorce is my 'free pass'. I should be going off and hooking up with lots of women, taking advantage of the situation.

Emma, on the other hand, is being advised that she is just the rebound partner; Grant will not settle down with her. All external inputs creating doubts. Be careful who you receive advice from, particularly when it is unsolicited. Opinions are like arseholes – everyone has one.

I was hard on the view that I would not bring any of the rubbish/baggage from my ex-wife into the relationship with Emma. That it would be disrespectful to both her and the relationship. She appeared wonderful and why couldn't or shouldn't things work? I was not going to over analyse this, her role, or her living in Melbourne as issues. I was going to be present.

Compared to what and according to whom were these issues? She was the first person I had been with since my (now-estranged) wife left. And so?

Emma was in a relationship with a married man. And so?

The relationship (if this was one) was between Emma and I. Everyone else was just providing peripheral noise. Emma phoned me the following weekend. She was at a wedding, wanting to know if we were serious or not. Thinking that there was some other suitor, I advised that I would like to see our relationship develop, and spend a very restless night on the GC in the process. My own insecurities were playing havoc with my imagination[31]. External influences.

We arranged to meet in Sydney in mid-November and spend a great weekend in the city together. Things were fresh, clean, no history, no baggage (except for my estranged wife). We were present. We laughed at Emma being my 'mistress'.

I went to South Africa in December and spent Christmas with Mum and Nic at Kleinemonde. It was hard not to disclose the

---

[31] Nothing happened. There was no other suitor that night. That was all in my head. Everyone at the wedding was very excited to hear about Emma's budding romance and she spent a wonderful evening with her friend Katie, who we miss dearly.

budding romance and my feelings for Emma to them. I feared they would think I was crazy for having such strong feelings for someone so soon after the estranged wife drama. We went out for dinner one night in East London to the restaurant where Karen used to work – Le Petit. As we arrive, the hostess excitedly greeted us and asked where she is. It was awkward, replying that things did not work out. It was another unprompted reminder of the failed fairy tale, a trigger reminding me of the past and the betrayal.

During the meal, I needed to leave the restaurant for a period to get some fresh air, fearing an anxiety attack.

CHAPTER TWELVE

2011 AND ONWARDS AND UPWARDS

After a great trip back to the homeland, I landed back in Australia in early January 2011. I was greeted with a voice message from Mike. I called him back and he stated that my ice-smoking drug-distributing neighbour has finally been busted. The police stopped him in his car and found an unlicensed gun hidden under the seat. A subsequent home inspection uncovered the meth lab, all detailed on page six of the Gold Coast Bulletin. It was late afternoon and I was at Sydney Airport. I tried to find a copy of the Bulletin at both the international and domestic terminals with no luck. A few hours later, I landed on the GC and after driving forty-five minutes home, I reached my neighbourhood after the sun had set. Suddenly, I noticed a huge 4x4 truck driving aggressively behind me.

I was one street and 400 metres from home, so I pulled over as they skidded past, tyres screeching, up my road and sped away. Following from a safe distance, I saw the vehicle pull into the driveway opposite mine. Great, ice-addict's friends were now going through the house/meth lab after the cops went through it yesterday. What was I to do?

I opened the garage door, drove in and quickly got out the car. I couldn't close the garage door quickly enough. Those looked like big, fired-up men getting out of that truck. I called Crime Stoppers to report it. Crime Stoppers had no details of the house and wanted me to walk outside to get the registration number of the 4x4 – no chance.

From the safety of my home, I could see them climbing into the garage roof and after spending half an hour at the place, they got back in the truck and sped off. Welcome back to the Gold Coast!

The next day, I went surfing with Ross and Dale at Fingal Beach in New South Wales. It was only the second time I had surfed there and for the second time, I would see a shark. There would be no third surf session at Fingal.

Later in the day, I flew to Melbourne to see Emma for her thirtieth birthday party. Talk about an international and interstate jet setter! After a big weekend, in what would become the norm, I caught an early morning flight from Melbourne home.

The rest of January 2011 would be heavily impacted by the floods that hit southeast Queensland. Lives would be lost and various Brisbane offices would be closed for weeks as the Brisbane River broke its banks, with the CBD badly impacted.

Apart from the floods, the January and February adventures also included putting the house on the market. The 'tropical Balinese oasis' had to go. Selling a house is seldom fun. Everything needs to be kept in immaculate shape in case a buyer wants to see it at the drop of a hat. The market was soft and after multiple viewings, a firm offer on the house was made, $5000 less than what we paid for it four years earlier. Interestingly, the house was bought and sold on the same day, four years apart.

After all the good work I did within the firm, I was transferred south to the head office in Sydney. From little old East London to the big smoke of Sydney! And I had once thought Brisbane was too big. Emma joined me from Melbourne just over a year later when her work transfer to the Sydney domestic terminal came through. We lived in an amazing sub-penthouse waterfront apartment in Pyrmont while my career in professional services blossomed.

I was promoted, nominated and accepted onto PwC's Young Leadership Team (YLT), a two-year professional development course for the top forty managers and senior managers in Australia, identified as potential future partners of the firm. The following year, my role was made redundant for the second time in my career. It would not be the last. The CFO stated that it is one of the best things about the YLT course – it empowered people to continue their current chosen path or to take the road less travelled, as I had to. Another redundancy, another breakup of sorts. It can be hard not to take personally. Unfortunately, the YLT course was removed from the learning and development curriculum the following year by the incoming CEO.

When the divorce was finalised, Emma and I went to South Africa for the third time, in March 2013. The previous trips were straight to the Eastern Cape, including East London, Grahamstown, Port Alfred and a few game reserves. This time we ventured down the Garden Route and to Cape Town, a truly beautiful part of the country. I picked up an engagement ring in Pretoria and travelled with it in my backpack everywhere we went, to the extent that I looked like the original European tourist (nothing like a stereotype!). I had grand plans of proposing on Table Mountain, only to have them dashed by every man and his dog getting there before me – it being the day after the Two Oceans Marathon. We went south into the National Park instead and after warning Emma all day about the baboons and how dangerous they were, I could not get her out the car to pop the question. Geez, why did it have to be so hard?

After much coaxing, Emma got out the car and we walked

onto a rocky ledge, not a baboon in sight. It was cold. It was windy. The place was originally called the Cape of Storms for a reason. In my nervousness in getting on one knee and popping the question, I ripped the engagement ring box in half. She said 'yes' and the celebrations began. Heading into the hotel bar on our return, I excitedly told the barman of our engagement as I ordered two Absolut Vodka shots (to reminisce about the night we met on Fraser Island years earlier – ever the romantic). The barman turned around and I read his name badge. 'Phil' – Dad's name. You could not make it up.

With cash from the redundancy in hand and a fiancé, in late November 2013, Emma and I got married in Noosa and honeymooned in Hawaii in December. We went to Fiji in January 2014 and found out we were pregnant while I was still unemployed.

Unable to find employment in Melbourne or Sydney for four months, I started a new career in the waste industry in Brisbane in March 2014. Emma remained based out of Sydney Airport so we lived apart for a few months, waiting for her transfer to come through. For a period, she lived in shared accommodation in a big fall from grace from the waterfront apartment in Sydney's inner west. Our first born (Lola Violet) arrived on her own at 11.17 p.m. on my dad's birthday later that year. Now we do celebrate 12 October – for both Lola and Dad! Our second child, Pearl Phillipa, arrived two years later, first name after the greatest rock band of the 1990s, and the second in memory of Dad.

We bought a townhouse in the inner west of Brisbane. I changed roles and was made redundant again. It appeared that I could not buy a permanent role, despite my best efforts and applying for literally hundreds of jobs. I began co-hosting a podcast called 'Flawless', where a host or a guest nominates an album they believe to be flawless. It was once huge in Kazakhstan and has now had over 30,000 listens, with over 130 episodes. The forum empowered me to talk about the impact the Matchbox Twenty album had on my life, helping me deal with the trauma of the car accident[32]. It helped me write this book too.

After attending a Resilience and Change session at work, I now facilitate various learning and development sessions as part of my consultancy firm. I have since facilitated courses for listed companies, councils, aged care services and state-owned corporations. It has begun to define my career. It may well become my career. I am also entertaining the idea of studying to become a psychologist, which I have put on hold while I complete this book.

However, sometimes one needs to put the studying aside and get busy doing.

---

[32] Have a listen to Flawless Episode 26 Matchbox 20 – Yourself or Someone Like You (https://flawlessamp.podbean.com/e/26-matchbox-20-yourself-or-someone-like-you/) to hear me discussing the album and the impact it had.

Emma and I got married in Noosa on 30th November 2013.
It was an amazing day filled with love and happiness. And… rain!

Emma, Lola, Pearl and I on holiday in Noosa - January 2023.

CONCLUSION

I commenced this book with the intention of providing you with the ambition to be a better human and clarity on who you are. I hoped detailing my experiences would provide an alternate perspective/narrative to the events that have shaped you and the life story you tell.

So, what have these significant life experiences provided me? What have I learned in the years since experiencing these four very different traumas? This is where I feel the real value of my experiences is.

It is naïve to think that there is one 'cure-all' solution that can be quickly applied to your set of life experiences and current situation. Life exists in the greys. It is seldom black or white. I will merely attempt to explain how I have tried to navigate through these experiences.

I believe that running from (or not fully acknowledging) your particular experiences is a futile exercise. You cannot escape your experiences, merely deal with them better. I am not my 'best self' around the 14th of April each year. I can get emotional and even fragile if I witness dogs fighting. I don't particularly like watching movies about betrayal, or those involving car crashes. I miss South Africa occasionally, particularly over the December holiday period. This is me, and that is fine. Acknowledge your set of circumstances, grasp the nettle and look forward.

One of the first items to address is the experience itself and the collateral damage that goes with it. Own the story, because you can absolutely bet that if you don't own it, it will own you. Owning the story can be as simple as crafting one sentence detailing what happened, the facts of the matter and removing any emotional state that you could attach to it. As an example, my line is: 'When I was nineteen, I was the driver in a car accident in which my father passed away.'

That is the gist of it. Sure, I could add more graphic detail to it. Yes, other family members were injured in the accident. Yes, I have experienced other events; however, that car accident occurred at a critical time of my physical and mental development. In my case, there has also been significant value gained through documenting the other experiences. This takes time. And refining. I am not sure there is a better way to do this than with a pen a paper through journalling.

Own your story, or it will own you.

There are also ways to better manage yourself on a day-to-day basis as part of your daily routine. Are you getting enough sleep? Sleep helps with recovery and most adults need seven to nine hours a night. It is unlikely you will be able to cope with less than that amount over an extended period.

Are you exercising enough? Numerous studies have proven that exercise creates good chemicals in your body, improving mood and overall wellbeing.

Are you eating correctly? For me personally, reducing carbohydrates significantly improved my mood and decreased my occasional bouts of anxiety. Almost everyone could afford to reduce their carbohydrate intake, as well as highly processed foods. Don't take my word on it, try it for yourself.

Are you cultivating a <u>life-long approach to learning</u>? I have always been a reader, from the comic books and Mad magazines that my mum used to collect to Roald Dahl and on to personal development books. Many of the books that have influenced me are listed in the Reference section of this book. I have read very little fiction over the past twenty years, the notable exceptions being *The Alchemist* by Paulo Coelho and *The Four Agreements* by Don Miguel Ruiz. More recently, I have made notes on these books. While occasionally tedious, this practice has been invaluable in reviewing books and documenting key themes from them. For the sake of completeness, a summary of four specific books that have had more of an influence on me follows in Appendix One. These books confirmed or endorsed previously held belief systems or significantly changed them. They have provided me with my code, if you will. If my stories have resonated with you at all, I encourage you to read them yourself.

For me, it comes down to two concepts, or themes: **Choice** and **Responsibility**.

Choice

You will experience bad days and you will experience better days in your life. External events will occur that are beyond your control – that you have limited or no influence over whatsoever. What you do have control over is how you <u>choose to frame and feel about these events</u>. When these events occur, do you choose to view them as permanent and pervasive? Have you personalised it?

Or do you choose to frame these events as temporary and contained, relating to other people's influences or events outside your control?

<u>Hint:</u> it is almost always temporary and contained and relates to circumstances beyond your control. Thank you to Martin Seligman for this insight.

Over the course of time, many, many wise people have stated

words to the effect of: 'It is what it is, I choose the response.'

Viktor Frankl most famously stated: 'Between stimulus and response there is space. In that space is our power to choose our response. In our response lies our growth and our freedom.' The stoics of yesteryear made similar statements. We control our response to events (both 'good' and 'bad'). How we choose to respond, if at all, is our <u>CHOICE</u>. Which is relevant because one does not always have to respond. One does not have to have an opinion about a topic.

It is my <u>choice</u> how to frame the traumas and the triumphs of my life and which adjectives I choose to describe these events. Each of the traumas could have been worse, significantly worse, and they are part of me, etched into my being for better or worse. I cannot escape them, as you cannot escape yours, should you have them. Furthermore, just because these bad events have happened does not mean similar events won't happen again. Experiencing traumatic events in the past does not exclude you from potentially experiencing ones in the future. I have also had some amazing times that I'm not sure could have been any better. This is the lens I choose to look through.

I chose the title of this book to be 'Yourself or Someone Like You' for two reasons:
- It was the title of the album I bought the day Dad passed, and
- because each of these traumatic events changed me.

I long to know the small child before he was mauled by that dog. I yearn for that loss of innocence. I long for the wisdom of my (paternal) father and the life that was taken so violently. I miss South Africa, my homeland. I wish the relationship with my first wife had ended differently. Betrayal and deception are horrible.

And while these events are a part of me, I have the opportunity every day to reconnect with that little boy and experience his childlike wonder of the world. To acknowledge that accidents happen, that people make mistakes and that countries change. In doing so, I find peace. These are my conscious choices in framing those events, and how to approach each day. In doing so, I maintain a positive outlook on life. Why? Because it is my CHOICE, and I do not like the alternative. Multiple studies have proven the positive impact an optimistic outlook has on longevity.

Each day you wake and in the main, you can choose how you feel. (I exclude those 'bad anniversary' days.) If you choose how you feel, why would you choose anything other than to feel great? I am not for a moment saying that you should only be in a positive state above all else. Experience the full range of human emotions, of course, but be careful how long you remain angry or spiteful. As Susan David states in her book *Emotional Intelligence*, having emotional agility is a valuable trait, as is acknowledging that <u>emotions are data and not direction</u>.

Responsibility

A word so seldomly used nowadays. I hear the word 'entitled' a lot more. 'I am entitled to this (*insert benefit/government grant/subsidy acknowledgement from society*). The world owes me something. Everyone is getting something; I deserve it too.'

However, who is actually responsible for your wellbeing? Who is responsible for your mental health? Who is responsible for your financial state? Who, ultimately, is responsible for you?

Not your parents (unless you are reading this as a very young child), not your friends, not your spouse or your government or society. Simply: <u>You</u>.

You have a duty to look after yourself. You are responsible for your decisions and the impact of those decisions. And guess what? You will not get it right all the time. You will make mistakes – we all do. We are human, and we need to take <u>responsibility</u>.

Take responsibility for your actions (or lack thereof). Look after yourself. Do your duty. Add value to your community. Generation upon generation of humans before you have evolved for us to arrive at this point in time. You are the latest version of thousands of years of refinement. You are the absolute best in a long line of humans that preceded you and just being here confirms you are a survivor.

You have Choice, and you have Responsibility; relish both.

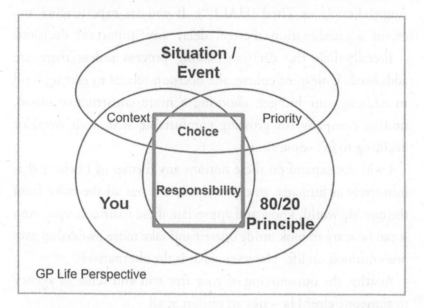

The diagram above illustrates my perspective. We experience Situations and Events daily and through factors unique to You, you add Context. The factors unique to you include but are not limited to your:

- Age
- Gender
- Culture
- Level of education
- Life experiences
- Values

- .Beliefs
- Ethnicity

I propose that it is our <u>Responsibility</u> to apply the <u>80/20 Principle</u>[33] in <u>Prioritising</u> the importance and relevance to these experiences. This in turn guides our <u>Choice</u> as to how to respond, if at all, to them.

I believe it really is that simple. Simple, but not easy. For example, this approach can be difficult to apply if one is Hungry, Angry, Lonely or Tired (HALT[34]). If you are experiencing any of, or a combination thereof, delay any important decisions – literally halt the decision-making process unless these are addressed. Unless, of course, the decision relates to getting food to address your hunger, choosing a more constructive mood, finding company (or growing comfortable with your own) or deciding to get some sleep.

I will not expand on these notions any further as I believe that intuitively as humans, when we finally cut out all the noise from the outside world, know and appreciate these basic concepts. And it can be scary to look inside oneself and take more ownership over one's outlook on life. However, what is the alternative?

Apathy, the outsourcing of your free will and sense of agency to someone else? Ha – not an option at all.

I hope that reading about my experiences has been a valuable use of your time. I believe once you start owning the narrative of your life, it will improve beyond measure. Refine your story and begin to tell it; I am sure your loved ones would love to hear it. And by all means, apply the GP Life Perspective to your own. I would appreciate any feedback.

Wishing you peace and power on your journey… wherever it may lead.

---

[33] Refer to Appendix One for more details on the 80/20 Principle.

[34] This approach also forms part of various recovery and twelve steps programs.

EPILOGUE

Writing this book changed me. And no doubt we are always changing regardless. It was hard to write. I didn't want to recall and then document certain events, whether I viewed them as happy or traumatic at the time I experienced them. It was incredibly hard recalling the passing of Dad, as it was recalling and detailing the many happy times I had with my first wife. It required deep introspection, which was at times confronting.

I am better for enduring the process. On some level, it was also deeply cathartic.

The initial intention, or reference for success even, was just to make a difference for one person. To prompt and encourage stories to be told that had for too long been pushed aside, buried, or carried as a burden deemed too dark or scary to share. Or even worse, deemed not relevant or traumatic enough, as can be the case with young males in particular. My thought process was that if I could help just one person, this exercise could be deemed a success.

However, by simply talking about this book and its content, I have already achieved that goal. Through sharing the high-level content at staff meetings, around the barbeque and other social gatherings, family and friends have shared stories with me that they had long kept buried. My heart is fuller for hearing these stories, as I believe their hearts are lighter for sharing them. There is a closeness that develops through allowing yourself to be vulnerable.

Perhaps this means that I aimed too low in trying to make an impact? This does not matter. Change can start small. Truthfully, it is all a bonus from here on out.

It reminds me of *The Star Thrower* by Loren Eiseley, adapted here. An old man was walking along a deserted beach at sunrise, the morning after a huge storm. The beach was littered with starfish up and down the beach as far as the eye could see. As he walked along, he began to see a figure in the distance. Moving closer, the old man noticed a young boy walking up to the high tide mark, leaning down, picking something up, walking back to the water's edge and throwing it out into the water. Up to the high tide mark again, back down to the water's edge, then throwing something into the ocean. Over and over... up and down the bay.

Approaching even closer, the old man noticed that the boy was picking up starfish and returning them to the ocean, one at a time. Perplexed, the old man approached the boy and said, 'Good morning, young lad' enthusiastically. 'May I ask what you are doing?'

'I am throwing starfish into the ocean,' replied the boy, smiling. 'The rough seas and high tide washed them up onto the beach and the starfish cannot get back to the water by themselves. As the sun rises, they will begin to die.'

'Ah,' said the old man, 'but there must be tens of thousands of starfish on this beach alone, let alone the other bays up and down this coastline. While your intention is admirable, can't you see that you really couldn't make much of a difference?'

The young boy smiled again, bent down and picked up another starfish. Throwing it back into the ocean as far as he possibly could, he replied, 'Made a difference to that one!'

You too can make a difference to that one person. Please do so. Thank you.

APPENDIX ONE

1. *The Resilience Project* by Hugh Van Cuylenburg

Hugh's experiences and research led him to the conclusion that more resilient people practice three activities every day: Gratitude, Empathy and Mindfulness, or GEM. His statistics about the state of mental health in Australia are staggering. We spend forty-nine per cent of our day thinking about the future and thirty-four per cent thinking about the past. The remainder, a mere sixteen per cent, is spent being present, thinking about what is happening in front of us as it is actually happening[35].

But how does one who has experienced trauma do that? How does one practice Gratitude, Empathy and Mindfulness after having experienced traumatic events? Surely this is easier said than done?

I am able to practice Gratitude because I made a conscious choice to look for the positives in the events I have experienced. Can I practice Empathy? Every day... I can empathise with children who have lost their parents, spouses whose partners have betrayed them, car crash victims and migrants. Can I practice Mindfulness, the state of being aware of the present

---

[35] Per interview with Spencer Howson on 4BC on 13/3/2022.

moment, calmly acknowledging and accepting one's feelings, thoughts and bodily sensations? Yes. And here is a hint: start by putting away your phone.

2. *The 80/20 Principle* by Richard Koch
Richard's book expertly details the Pareto Principle and discusses the observation that approximately eighty per cent of consequences come from twenty per cent of causes. Life is imbalanced. We put different values on different events. The observation is relevant across all realms of life. Examples include:

- There are the big four accounting firms that generate the lion's share of revenue in that market, and then the remaining practises. Within those institutions, the partners again earn the majority of what is distributed. The same principle applies in most other industries. The same applies to the C-Suite of listed companies, with those C-Suite roles earning multiples of what the lowest-paid employee would earn. You could look at the mobile phone industry, with Apple and Samsung owning by far the majority of the market, and then the others. Or fast food with McDonald's, or Pepsi and Coke and then all other soft drink manufacturers. It applies to sporting apparel. Sports matches are turned in a single moment (a few seconds or minutes) over an eighty or ninety-minute period. The same for the movies that you watch. You can probably quote an iconic line from your favourite movie, mere seconds in a ninety-minute-plus experience making up the entire film.
- You get far more value from certain daily activities than others; for example, walking on the beach for an hour

as opposed to being stuck in traffic. Spending time with your family as opposed to balancing another bank reconciliation. Even your shopping list contains some items that are more important than others... you can afford to forget the spices or the Nando's sauce but don't dare forget the bread and milk!

The world is imbalanced – how are you taking advantage of this fact?

This principle applies absolutely to the 14th of April for me. One day each year that still has more influence over me than others. It remains easily my toughest day each year. My period of reflection. I have managed to compress the period of influence from a month before and after that date to a few days, around 13 to 15 April each year. That compression process took years, and some years I have been more successful than others. It took years of patience (and frustration and tolerance, I would think) from girlfriends and wives. I did not like me during these periods. I did not like anyone... I have since made a conscious decision that I do not want to waste too much of my life mourning and wallowing in the trauma of that accident. Three days (ish) is what I will give that event each year. I also take these few days off work each year to reflect.

And again, in reviewing the other traumas and applying the Pareto Principle, those events could have been worse: I could have lost an eye during the dog attack. The dog could have injured Mum, Richard and me. I could have been the sole survivor in that car accident. Dad may have survived, but with brain damage and been wheelchair-bound. I have chosen to focus on the twenty per cent that did not go bad as opposed to the eighty per cent that did.

3. *The Body Keeps the Score* by Bessel van der Kolk

It was not until reading this book that I fully appreciated the impact and significance of the dog attack when I was three years old. Bessel 'uses recent scientific advances to show how trauma literally reshapes both body and brain, compromising sufferers' capacities for pleasure, engagement, self-control, and trust. He explores innovative treatments—from neurofeedback and meditation to sports, drama, and yoga—that offer new paths to recovery by activating the brain's natural neuroplasticity.'

If you have experienced trauma, this book will help you better understand yourself. It is a tough read, and worth it.

4. *The Four Agreements* by Don Miguel Ruiz

A book so good it is worth reading annually. It is a short, easy read. Applying the Four Agreements to my life has significantly improved my overall wellbeing, as well as my relationships. The Four Agreements are:

1. <u>Be impeccable with your word</u> – Speak with integrity, saying only what you mean. Do not use the spoken word to gossip about others or to speak against yourself. Use your words for truth and love.

2. <u>Do not make assumptions</u> – Find the courage to ask open questions and state what you really want. Communicate as clearly as you can with others to avoid misunderstandings, sadness and unnecessary drama.

3. <u>It's not personal</u> – People are not against you. People are for themselves! What people do and say is a projection of their reality. When you become immune to (or ignore) the opinions and actions of others, you will cease being the victim of needless suffering. There are genuinely very few

people in your life whose opinion you should care about.

4. <u>Always do your best</u> – And accept that your best will change from moment to moment. If you are ill or haven't slept well, your performance will be hindered. By always doing your best you avoid regret, self-judgement and self-abuse.

This is especially relevant during the anniversary periods of traumatic events, such as a loved one's passing. Be gentle on yourself during these times.

BOOK REFERENCES

1. Richard Koch – *The 80/20 Principle*
    (https://www.goodreads.com/book/show/181206.
    The_80_20_Principle)

2. Dr. Susan David – *Emotional Agility*
    (https://www.amazon.com.au/Emotional-Agility-Unstuck-
    Embrace-Change/dp/0241976588/)

3. Sir Ken Robinson – *The Element*
    (https://www.sirkenrobinson.com/product/the-element-
    how-finding-your-passion-changes-everything/)

4. Rosamund Stone Zander and Benjamin Stander – *The Art of
    Possibility*
    (https://www.booktopia.com.au/the-art-of-possibility-
    benjamin-zander/book/9780142001103.html)

5. Paulo Coelho – *The Alchemist*
    (https://www.booktopia.com.au/the-alchemist-25th-
    anniversary-paulo-coelho/book/9780062315007.html)

6. Brené Brown – *Dare to Lead*
    (https://www.booktopia.com.au/dare-to-lead-bren-brown/
    book/9781785042140.html)

7. Ryan Holiday and Stephen Hanselman – *The Daily Stoic* (https://www.booktopia.com.au/the-daily-stoic-ryan-holiday/book/9780735211735.html)

8. Bessel van der Kolk – *The Body Keeps the Score* (https://www.booktopia.com.au/the-body-keeps-the-score-bessel-van-der-kolk/book/9780143127741.html)

9. Simon Sinek – *Start With Why* (https://www.amazon.com.au/Start-Why-Leaders-Inspire-Everyone/dp/0241958229/)

10. Carol Dweck – *Mindset* (https://www.booktopia.com.au/mindset-carol-dweck/book/9781472139955.html)

11. Martin Seligman – *Authentic Happiness* (https://www.booktopia.com.au/authentic-happiness-martin-seligman/book/9781864713022.html)

12. Jeff Olson – *The Slight Edge* (https://www.booktopia.com.au/the-slight-edge-jeff-olson/book/9781613398272.html)

13. Oprah Winfrey and Dr Bruce Perry – *What Happened to You?* (https://www.booktopia.com.au/what-happened-to-you--oprah-winfrey/book/9781529068474.html)

14. Rob Goffee and Gareth Jones – *Why Should Anyone Be Led by You?* (https://www.booktopia.com.au/why-should-anyone-be-led-by-you-with-a-new-preface-by-the-authors-rob-goffee/book/9781633697683.html)

15. Shawn Achor – *The Happiness Advantage* (https://www.booktopia.com.au/the-happiness-advantage-shawn-achor/book/9780307591555.html)

16. James Clear – *Atomic Habits*
(https://www.booktopia.com.au/atomic-habits-james-clear/book/9781847941831.html)

17. David Epstein – *Range*
(https://www.booktopia.com.au/range-david-epstein/book/9781509843527.html)

18. Viktor Frankl – *Man's Search for Meaning*
(https://www.booktopia.com.au/man-s-search-for-meaning-viktor-e-frankl/book/9781846041242.html)

19. Loren Eiseley – *The Star Thrower*
(https://www.amazon.com/gp/product/0156849097)

Shawline Publishing Group Pty Ltd
www.shawlinepublishing.com.au

SHAWLINE
PUBLISHING
GROUP

More great Shawline titles can be found by scanning the QR code below.
New titles also available through Books@Home Pty Ltd.
Subscribe today at www.booksathome.com.au or scan the QR code below.